nihongo notes 5

studying japanese in context

by
osamu mizutani
nobuko mizutani

The Japan Times, Ltd.

First edition: July 1983
Third printing: March 1985

Jacket design by Koji Detake

ISBN4-7890-0210-1

Published by The Japan Times, Ltd.
5-4, Shibaura 4-chome, Minato-ku, Tokyo 108, Japan

Printed in Japan

FOREWORD

This book is a compilation of the 70 columns which appeared in *The Japan Times* from December 13, 1981, to April 10, 1983, under the title "Nihongo Notes." (The preceding 280 columns have been published as Nihongo Notes 1, 2, 3 and 4.)

It is a great pleasure for us to be able to publish another volume of "Nihongo Notes," and we are grateful to you for your continued interest. We hope that you will enjoy reading it and find it of some help in understanding Japanese as it is used in Japanese society.

In this volume, while continuing to explain the actual usage of various Japanese expressions, we have attempted to take up more specific situations and to provide more detailed explanations. The columns in this volume include various expressions of reserve and consideration used toward the listener, and also several common mistakes that foreigners are apt to make.

For the convenience of the reader, we have added a list of the words and phrases discussed in all five volumes of "Nihongo Notes" as well as an index to important expressions classified according to usage.

We would like to acknowledge the help of Janet Ashby, who checked the English for these columns and offered valuable suggestions just as she did for the preceding four volumes.

June, 1983
Osamu and Nobuko Mizutani

CONTENTS

Soo-deshoo-ka (I wonder) 8

Chigaimasu (You're wrong) 10

Ashita-ni shitara doo-desu-ka (Why don't you
    make it tomorrow?) 12

Ichido ome-ni kakaritai-to omoimasu (I'd like
    to see you sometime) 14

Watashi-niwa muzukashii-desu (It's difficult
    for me) 16

Sorede . . . (And so . . .) 18

Ii-ja arimasen-ka (Isn't it all right?) 20

Otaku-de ii-desu (Your house will do) 22

Naanda, kimi-ka (Oh, it's you!) 24

Shitsuree-desu-ga . . . (Excuse me, but . . .) 26

Ato-de denwa-o kakemasu (I'll call him later) 28

Ohikitome-shimashite . . . (I'm sorry I
    detained you so long) 30

Joozu-desu-ne (You do it very well) 32

Naorimashita (It has been repaired).............. 34

Sore-ga . . . (That . . .) 36

Kekkon-shite-imasu (She's married) 38

Iku-n-da-tte? (Did you say he's going?) 40

Soo-desu-yone (That's certainly so, isn't it?). 42

Kekkon-suru soo-desu (I hear she's getting
    married)... 44

Osoku narimashite . . . (I'm sorry I'm late) .. 46

Kore, tsutsunde (Wrap this, will you?) 48

Sonna koto arimasen-tara (That's not so!) 50

Sumimasen, osoku natte (I'm sorry to be
    late) 52

Irasshaimase (I'm glad you have come)......... 54

Ashi-o fumaremashita (Someone stepped on
    my foot)... 56

Sen-en-ni narimasu (That will be ¥1,000) 58
Soo-kamo shiremasen (That may be so) 60
Shochuu omimai-mooshiagemasu (Summer
  Season Greetings) 62
Moo yameru-n-da (Now stop it)..................... 64
Itte-kurereba yokatta-noni (You should have
  asked me).................................. 66
Maido arigatoo-gozaimasu (Thank you very
  much for your patronage) 68
Zuibun (Terribly) 70
Ki-ni suru koto-wa arimasen-yo (You don't
  have to worry about it) 72
Nemukute, nemukute . . . (I'm so sleepy)...... 74
Teeshoku-de ii-desu (Today's lunch will do) .. 76
Boku-mo (Me, too) 78
Koko-wa watashi-ga . . . (I will take care of
  this)... 80
Koko-ni kissaten-ga aru-desho? (There's a
  coffee shop here, you know?) 82
Kimura-san-desu (It's Mr. Kimura)................ 84
Kore, oishii-wane (This is good, isn't it?) 86
Kore-wa are-deshoo-ne . . . (This case is like
  that, isn't it?) 88
Gomen-kudasai (Excuse me) 90
Desu-ne (It is, isn't it?)............................. 92
Mite-itadakemasen-ka (Would you please take
  a look at this?)................................. 94
Osokatta-desu-ne (You're late) 96
Yasundara doo-desu-ka (Why don't you rest?) 98
"Kono" to "Sono" (This and that) 100
Gobusata-itashimashita (I'm sorry I have
  been neglecting to see you and write to
  you)... 102
Otoko-wa nyooboo-da (A man is a wife?)....... 104
Moo demashita (It has already left)................ 106
Kiree-ni taberu (To eat up) 108

5

Itte-mo ii-kedo . . . (I don't mind going, but
 . . .) 110
Bakari (About; Only) 112
Tomarimasu-ka (Are you going to stay
 overnight?) 114
Issho-ni shimashoo (Let's do it together) 116
Uchi-no akachan (Our baby) 118
Kanai (My wife) 120
Ii toshi (Good age) 122
Ii-desu-ne. Demo warui-desu-ne. (It's good,
 but it's bad) 124
Hee? (Really?) 126
Wakaru dokoro-ka . . . (Far from being able
 to understand . . .) 128
Yamada-san-de irasshaimasu-ka (Are you Mr.
 Yamada?) 130
Takaku nai-ja nai (It isn't expensive, is it?) 132
Zenbu-wa wakarimasen-deshita (I didn't
 understand all of it) 134
Yokka-kara-desu-ka (From the fourth?) 136
Doomo umaku dekinai (Somehow I can't do it
 well) 138
Tanaka-san-kara denwa-ga arimashita (There
 was a telephone call from Mr. Tanaka) 140
Ki-ni shinai, ki-ni shinai (Don't worry!) 142
"Tooka?" "Deshita." (The tenth? Yes.) 144
Kaetta hoo-ga ii (You had better go home) 146
GENERAL INDEX (Volumes 1-5) 149
Index to Words, Phrases and Sentences
 (Volumes 1-5) 157

Note Concerning Romanization

The romanization used in this book (as well as in *An Introduction to Modern Japanese*) is based on the Hepburn system with the following modifications.

1. When the same vowel occurs consecutively, the letter is repeated rather than using the "-" mark.
   ex. *Tookyoo* (instead of *Tōkyō*)
2. The sound indicated by the hiragana ん is written with "*n*" regardless of what sound follows it.
   ex. *shinbun* (instead of *shimbun*)
   ex. *shinpai* (instead of *shimpai*)

The words connected with hyphens are pronounced as one unit.
   ex. *genki-desu*
   ex. *Soo-desu-ne*

Soo-deshoo-ka
そうでしょうか
(I wonder)

Mr. Lerner has become able to handle daily conversation in Japanese fairly easily, but still finds difficult a few expressions that sound very similar but mean something very different. Just recently, Miss Yoshida and Mr. Lerner were listening to Mr. Okada complaining about his boss. Each time Mr. Okada explained how hurt he felt when he was treated unfairly, Miss Yoshida said

> *Soo-deshoo-ne.*
> そうでしょうね。
> (It must be so.)

Mr. Lerner knew that *Soo-deshoo-ne* is used to express one's sympathy, and he wanted to use it, too. But when he actually did, he inadvertently said

> *Soo-deshoo-ka.*
> そうでしょうか。
> (I wonder.)

Seeing Mr. Okada looking strange, and Miss Yoshida embarrassed, he suddenly felt as if he had not made any progress at all in Japanese.

*　　　*　　　*

To express one's sympathy toward someone with a problem, *Soo-desu-ne* is often used. For instance, when someone complains about his jet lag saying

> *Doomo mada atama-ga hakkiri-shimasen.*

(Somehow my head doesn't work right yet.)

you might say

> Soo-deshoo-ne.
> (It must be so.)

Sometimes *ne* is prolonged to emphasize the feeling of sympathy as in

> Honto-ni soo-deshoo-nee.
> (It must be so, indeed.)

On the other hand, *Soo-deshoo-ka* is used to imply doubt or criticism, as in

> A: *Ima-nara ma-ni au-deshoo.*
> (I think we can be in time if we start now.)
> B: *Soo-deshoo-ka. Michi-ga komimasu-yo.*
> (I wonder. The traffic will be heavy.)

Or, if someone says that a person is capable of doing some work and you say *Soo-deshoo-ka,* it can be an expression of opposition.

When trying to say *Soo-deshoo-ne,* Mr. Lerner might have used *Soo-deshoo-ka* by mistake because it sounds similar to *Soo-desu-ka* (Is that right?). *Soo-desu-ka* varies in nuance depending on the tone with which it is said, and it can sound sympathetic, but *Soo-deshoo-ka* cannot be used to express sympathy.

Chigaimasu
ちがいます
(You're wrong)

Last night Mr. Lerner tried to call an acquaintance on the phone, but must have somehow dialed the wrong number. The woman on the other end said

Chigaimasu.
ちがいます。
(You're wrong. — *lit.* It is different.)

He remembered that Miss Yoshida often uses *Chigaimasu* in conversation, not necessarily about something like a wrong telephone number. He had learned this expression as a synonym for *Iie* (No) a long time before, but he hadn't used it himself.

*　　　*　　　*

Chigaimasu is often used in place of *Iie* as well as with it. People say *Iie.*, *Chigaimasu.*, or *Iie, chigaimasu* depending on the situation.

It seems *Chigaimasu* is preferred when one wants to clearly tell someone that his statement is wrong. This is most often used when answering a question about factual information. For example, if you ask someone

Kono densha-wa kyuukoo-desu-ka.
(Is this train an express train?)

he will very likely reply in the negative with *Chigaimasu* or *Iie, chigaimasu.*
But when the question concerns a personal judgment or evaluation, *Chigaimasu* is usually

avoided. For instance, when you say *Kore-ga ichi-ban ii-to omoimasu-ga. . .* (I think this is the best. What do you think? — *lit.* I think this is the best, but. . .) the other person will probably use some expressions other than *Chigaimasu* to indicate his disagreement. This is quite similar to the use of *Iie*; the difference between *Iie* and *Chigaimasu* is that the latter sounds more definite, and *Iie, chigaimasu* is used when the speaker wants to emphasize his answer.

Chigaimasu is also used to point out a mistake pure and simple, like a clerk handing you something different from what you have asked for. You may say something like

Chigaimasu. Kore-ja arimasen.
ちがいます。これじゃ　ありません。
(This is not what I asked for.)

when the salesgirl has handed you a silver tie pin instead of a platinum one.

Ashita-ni shitara doo-desu-ka
あしたに したら どうですか
(Why don't you make it tomorrow?)

Yesterday evening Mr. Lerner and Mr. Takada asked Miss Yoshida to go drinking with them after work, but she said that she had to work overtime to finish the day's work. Mr. Lerner was about to say

Ashita-ni suru-to doo-desu-ka.

to mean "How about doing it tomorrow instead?," when Mr. Takada said

Ashita-ni shitara doo?
あしたに したら どう？

Mr. Lerner thought that Mr. Takada meant the same thing as he did, and wondered what difference there is between . . . *suru-to doo-desu-ka* and . . . *shitara doo-desu-ka.*

* * *

Ashita-ni suru-to doo-desu-ka also means "How will it be if you decide on tomorrow for it?" but this is a question about the result of making it tomorrow rather than actually suggesting making it tomorrow. If Mr. Lerner had asked this question, Miss Yoshida would have tried to explain what would happen, as in

Ashita-ni suru-to ma-ni awanaku naru-kamo shiremasen.
(If I postpone the work until tomorrow, I may not be able to finish it in time.)

12

On the other hand . . . *tara doo-desu-ka* is an expression for making suggestions. You might say, for instance, to someone who is working and looks very tired

Sukoshi yasundara doo-desu-ka.
(Why don't you rest a while?)

To make this expression more polite, you can say

Sukoshi oyasumi-ni nattara ikaga-desu-ka.
少し　お休みに　なったら　いかがですか。

Such other expressions as *Yasumeba ii-de-shoo* or *Yasumu-to ii-deshoo* can also be used to make suggestions, but *yasundara doo-desu-ka* sounds less pressing and more reserved. And the last part — *doo-desu-ka, ikaga-desu-ka,* or *doo* (familiar) — can be left out; in this case the first part will be said with a rising intonation.

Ichido ome-ni kakaritai-to omoimasu
一度 お目に かかりたいと 思います
(I'd like to see you sometime)

A Mr. Kimura called Mr. Lerner on the phone yesterday afternoon; he said that he was working on a certain project and wondered if Mr. Lerner could help him. After explaining the situation, he said

Ichido ome-ni kakaritai-to omoimasu-ga . . .
一度 お目に かかりたいと 思いますが……
(*lit.* I'd like to see you one time, but . . .)

Mr. Lerner told him when he would be available and hung up the phone, but he wondered why Mr. Kimura had said *Ichido* . . . (One time . . .) Did he want to see Mr. Lerner just once and no more?

*   *   *

The word *ichido* is often used to mean "sometime in the future" when making a proposal or request in a social situation. *Ichido ome-ni kakaritai* does not mean that the speaker is determined not to see the listener more than once. Rather, saying

Zehi ichido oide-kudasai means "Please come and see me by all means" or "You must come and see me sometime."

In a similar way *hitotsu* is also used to mean "some" when offering something or making a proposal as in

Hitotsu oagari-kudasai.
(Please have some.)

14

This *hitotsu* is also used in a request as in

    Hitotsu onegai-shimasu.

meaning "Please take care of this. Thank you."
Sometimes a person who accepts a request will
say

    Ja, hitotsu yatte-mimashoo.
    じゃ、ひとつ　やってみましょう。
    (Then I'll give it a try.)

These words *ichido* and *hitotsu* can be left out
as far as the meaning is concerned, but they
serve the function of making the intention of the
following speech clear at the beginning of the sentence, so the listener can get ready. The use of
this kind of word is especially recommended in
social situations; it will help avoid having your
Japanese sound abrupt.

Watashi-niwa muzukashii-desu
わたしには　むずかしいです
(It's difficult for me)

Mr. Lerner was invited by the Takadas to a New Year's celebration yesterday evening. After dinner, they played a traditional card game called *karuta*. It was a lot of fun, but Mr. Lerner found it rather difficult to listen to a proverb read aloud and then select the card with the first syllable of that proverb on it together with an illustration. When the play was over, Mr. Lerner said

Watashi-ni muzukashii-desu.

meaning "It's difficult for me." They understood, but Mr. Takada said he should say

Watashi-niwa muzukashii-desu.
わたしには　むずかしいです。

instead. Mr. Lerner wondered if there was that much difference between *watashi-ni* and *watashi-niwa*.

*　　　*　　　*

To mean "It is difficult for me," one should say *Watashi-niwa muzukashii-desu*; *Watashi-ni muzukashii-desu* sounds awkward. . . . *Niwa* should also be used instead of . . . *ni* to indicate whether something is advantageous or not to someone. For example, to indicate one's convenience one says

Watashi-niwa gogo-no hoo-ga tsugoo-ga ii-n-desu-ga. . .

16

(The afternoon is better for me.)

Or, to refer to something valuable to a person, one says

Ano-ko-niwa tomodachi-ga ichiban daiji-desu.
(To that child friends are the most important thing.)

To add the meaning of "also," . . .*nimo* is used as in

Gakusee-nimo kyooshi-nimo yasumi-wa arigatai mono-desu.
(Holidays are nice — *lit.* something one should be grateful for — for both students and teachers.)

Sometimes . . .*ni totte* is used to emphasize personal standpoint.

Watashi-ni totte nani-yori daijina mono-desu.
わたしに とって 何より 大事な ものです。
(This is more precious than anything to me.)

Sorede. . .
それで……
(And so. . .)

Mr. Kato, who had traveled in Europe during the holidays, was telling his colleagues about his trip. When he said that he had taken a wrong train in France, Miss Yoshida asked him

Sorede doo shimashita.
それで どう しました。
(And so, what did you do?)

Mr. Lerner had also wanted to ask this question, and he wondered if he could use *soshite* instead of *sorede.*

* * *

Mr. Lerner could have said *Soshite doo shimashita-ka,* but it would have sounded like a schoolboy's question in a classroom. In usual conversation, *sorede* is used to show the speaker's interest in knowing the development or outcome of some incident. Very often its shorter form *de* is used as in

A: *Tootoo ano-hito konakatta-n-desu-yo.*
   (He didn't show up at all.)
B: *De, doo narimashita.*
   (And what happened?)

Sorede is also used to connect related sentences or phrases as in

Kinoo-wa atama-ga itakute, sorede kaisha-o yasumimashita.
   (I had a headache so I stayed home from the

office yesterday.)

Sometimes *sorekara* (after that) is used to ask about further developments, but this emphasizes that the two incidents took place in consecutive order, as in

A: *Hajime-ni Kyooto-e itte-nee.*
   (I went to Kyoto first.)
B: *Sorekara. . .*
   (After that. . .?)
A: *Sorekara Nara-e itta-n-da-yo.*
   (Then I went to Nara.)

(Saying *sorede* or *sorekara* alone sounds personal and familiar, and should be avoided in polite conversation.)

On the other hand *soshite* (and) is appropriately used for connecting one's own phrases or sentences in expository statements or monologues rather than in conversation, where the speaker-listener relations are important.

Ii-ja arimasen-ka
いいじゃ　ありませんか
(Isn't it all right?)

Mr. Okada asked Mr. Lerner to have some beer after their business discussions yesterday evening. Mr. Lerner said that he had something to go over for work the next day and had to go home early, but Mr. Okada said

Ii-ja arimasen-ka.
いいじゃ　ありませんか。
(*lit.* Isn't it good?)

Mr. Lerner understood that Mr. Okada was insisting on treating him, but he did not know what was left out before *Ii-ja arimasen-ka*. He wondered if this usage was an expression used by a host to detain a guest.

*　　　*　　　*

Before *ii-desu* (it's all right) or *ii-ja arimasen-ka* (isn't it all right?) various phrases can be left out. Very often this is used to mean "you don't have to do it"; in this case *shinakute-mo* is understood and left out. A host often says to a guest who is going to leave

Ii-ja arimasen-ka.

to mean "You don't have to go yet, do you?"

In Mr. Okada's statement, something like *sonna-ni hatarakanakute-mo* (even if you don't work so hard) is left out. By *ii-ja arimasen-ka* he meant "You don't have to go home so early and work. Please be relaxed and be my guest." This phrase is said especially often to someone who is hesitating about accepting an offer. For example, a host tries to fill the sake cup of his guest, and the guest says

Guest: *Moo takusan itadakimashita.*
(I have had plenty.)
Host: *Maa, ii-ja arimasen-ka.*

Here the host means "Please don't be so reserved."

This expression is also used when comforting someone; in this case *shinpai shinakute-mo* (even if you don't worry) is left out before *ii-ja arimasen-ka.* For example, to a father who is complaining that his son doesn't study much, one may say something like

Ii-ja arimasen-ka. Sono-uchi yaru ki-ni narimasu-yo.
(Don't worry. He will start to feel like studying before long.)

In any case, *ii-ja arimasen-ka* is said with a falling tone since it is not a real question, and usually *ii* is pronounced higher than *arimasen-ka.*

Otaku-de ii-desu
おたくで いいです
(Your house will do)

Mr. Lerner and Miss Yoshida were planning a party for Mr. Kimura, who is going to get married soon. When they were discussing where to have the party, Mr. Mori, the director of the company, came in and said

Boku-no uchi-de ii-kane.
ぼくの うちで いいかね。
(Will my house do?)

Miss Yoshida looked surprised and pleased. Mr. Lerner was also very glad to hear that, so he said

Ee, otaku-de ii-desu.
ええ、おたくで いいです。
(Yes, your house will do.)

Miss Yoshida hurriedly said something like "That would be more than ideal but wouldn't it be trouble for your family?" as if to cover up Mr. Lerner's blunder.

*　　　*　　　*

Several expressions can be used to make a proposal. Such expressions as . . . *wa doo-desu-ka* and . . . *ga ii-deshoo* are often used, and these expressions sound more confident about the speaker's judgment than . . . *de ii-desu-ka*. The expression . . . *de ii-desu-ka* implies that the speaker is afraid that the offer may not be very good but he will be happy if it can be accepted; it therefore sounds more modest and reserved.

When . . . *de ii-desu-ka* is used in a situation where the speaker's personal interest is not involved, it can be used in the answer too, as in *Ee, . . . de ii-desu.* For instance, when two people are discussing where to meet next time, both of them can use this expression, as in

A: *Shinjuku-de ii-desu-ka.*
   (Will Shinjuku do?)
B: *Ee, Shinjuku-de ii-desu.*
   (Yes, Shinjuku will be fine.)

Or, B could say *Ee, sore-de ii-desu* or *Ee, sore-de kekkoo-desu* (Yes, that will be fine.)

But when the offer involves the personal interests of the person who makes it, the person who accepts it will avoid using . . . *de ii-desu.* For instance, if someone says, while showing you a letter of introduction he has written for you,

Doo-desu-ka. Kore-de ii-desu-ka.

you should avoid using . . . *de ii-desu.* Rather, you should thank him by saying something like

Ee, honto-ni arigatoo-gozaimashita.
(Yes, thank you very much.)

This is especially true when you want to speak politely to someone offering you something.

Naanda, kimi-ka
なあんだ、君か
(Oh, it's you!)

Mr. Lerner and Mr. Takada were talking at lunchtime, when the telephone rang. Mr. Lerner answered it, and the operator told him that a Mr. Suzuki wanted to talk to Mr. Takada. Mr. Takada did not remember who Mr. Suzuki was, and said very politely

Hai, Takada-de gozaimasu.
(This is Mr. Takada speaking.)

But the next moment he completely changed his tone and said

Naanda, kimi-ka.
なあんだ、君か。
(Oh, it's you!)

and started talking in a very familiar manner. It was as if he were talking to two different persons.

* * *

It is customary to start speaking politely when you don't know to whom you are talking on the telephone. In Mr. Takada's case, since there are so many Suzukis, at first he did not know who was calling him, and he started talking politely. The expression *Naanda* is used when you are surprised and realize that you don't have to worry about something. For instance, if you mistakenly think that you have lost your wallet and then find it in an unexpected place, you will say

24

Naanda, konna tokoro-ni atta.
(Oh, it was here!)

Mr. Takada was surprised to find that Mr. Suzuki was an old friend of his and felt relieved from formality.

When you call a good friend or someone you can talk with in a familiar manner, and a member of his family answers the phone, you should refer to your friend politely as in

Moshi-moshi, Makoto-san irasshaimasu-ka.
もしもし、まことさん　いらっしゃいますか。
(Hello, is Makoto home?)

Even if you usually call him "Makoto" when talking with him, you should add *-san* when talking with his family members. In a similar way, if you call a good friend at work and someone else answers the phone, it is polite to use a term of respect as in

Yamamoto-sensee irasshaimasu-ka.
(Is Professor Yamoto there?)
or
Kawakami-san oide-ni narimasu-ka.
(Is Mr. Kawakami there?)

Shitsuree-desu-ga . . .
失礼ですが······
(Excuse me, but . . .)

Mr. Lerner was talking with Mr. Mori, the director of the company, in his office yesterday afternoon. In the course of the conversation he wanted to ask Mr. Mori what university he had graduated from, so he started by saying

    Ano, shitsuree-shimasu-ga . . .

meaning "Excuse me, but . . ." (*lit.* I'm going to be rude, but . . .) Then Mr. Mori stood up from his chair and said

    Ja, mata.
    (Well, see you later.)

as if he were leaving. Mr. Lerner did not understand exactly, but felt that something must have been wrong with his Japanese.

      *   *   *

Instead of *shitsuree-shimasu-ga*, Mr. Lerner should have used *shitsuree-desu-ga* and then completed his question as in

    Ano, shitsuree-desu-ga, dochira-no daigaku-o ode-ni narimashita-ka.
    (Excuse me, but from which university did you graduate?)

When you want to ask someone a personal question, you should first say *shitsuree-desu-ga* as in

    Shitsuree-desu-ga, Tanaka-san-de irasshai-

masu-ka?

(Excuse me, are you Mr. Tanaka?)

Shitsuree-desu-ga, okusan-wa Nihon-no kata-desu-ka.

(Excuse me, but is your wife a Japanese?)

To make the expression even more polite you can add *makoto-ni* as in

> *Makoto-ni shitsuree-desu-ga . . .*
> まことに　失礼ですが……
> (This is a very rude question, but . . .)

On the other hand *Shitsuree-shimasu* literally means "I'm going to be rude," and is used when you are going to perform some action, such as sitting down, leaving the room, or picking up something. For instance, when the host says *Doozo okake-kudasai* (Please sit down), the visitor will say either *Hai, arigatoo-gozaimasu* or *Shitsuree-shimasu* before sitting down. Or, when someone hands you a letter saying *Doozo goran-kudasai* (Please take a look at it), it is polite for you to say *Shitsuree-shimasu* before actually reading the letter. Therefore it is natural that Mr. Mori thought that Mr. Lerner was leaving when he said *Shitsuree-shimasu.*

Ato-de denwa-o kakemasu
あとで 電話を かけます
(I'll call him later)

Yesterday afternoon Mr. Lerner was trying to make an appointment with Mr. Okada on the phone. Mr. Okada wasn't sure of his schedule yet and said that he would call him back later. So when Miss Yoshida asked him about it, Mr. Lerner told her

Ato-de denwa-o kakemasu.
あとで 電話を かけます。

meaning "He'll call me later." But after a while Miss Yoshida came again and asked him if he had called Mr. Okada yet; it was as if she thought that Mr. Lerner was going to call Mr. Okada. Mr. Lerner wondered if he should have said *Okada-san-wa ato-de denwa-o kakemasu* without leaving out the subject of the sentence.

      *   *   *

Some foreigners wonder if the Japanese do not sometimes misunderstand each other when they leave out the subject of a sentence, but they usually don't because the subject is left out according to rules.

One rule is that when answering a question the subject mentioned in the question is usually omitted, as in

A: *Tanaka-san-wa itsu kimasu-ka.*
   (When will Mr. Tanaka come?)
B: *Ashita kimasu.*
   (He'll come tomorrow.)

In B's sentence, *Tanaka-san-wa* or *Kare-wa* (he) or *Ano-hito-wa* (that person) is not mentioned unless it is particularly emphasized.

Another rule is that sometimes the subject is indicated by use of specific respectful or humble verbs as in

A: *Itsu irasshaimasu-ka.*
   (When will you/he/she/they come?)
B: *Ashita mairimasu.*
   (I'll come tomorrow.)
or
B: *Ashita irasshaimasu.*
   (He/She/They will come tomorrow.)

One more rule is that when there is no other subject indicated either verbally or by the situation, the subject of the sentence is the speaker himself. Therefore, in Mr. Lerner's case above, when he said *Ato-de denwa-o kakemasu,* naturally Miss Yoshida took this to mean "I'll call him later."

What Mr. Lerner should have done is either (1) indicate that he was reporting what he had heard from Mr. Okada, as in:

Ato-de denwa-kakeru-to iimashita.
(He said he would call me later.)
Ato-de denwa-o kakeru soo-desu.
(I understand he will call me later.)

or (2) indicate that the action of calling is directed toward him, as in:

Ato-de denwa-o kakete-kimasu.
(He's going to call me.)

Ohikitome-shimashite. . .
おひきとめしまして……
(I'm sorry I detained you so long)

The other day Mr. Lerner and Mr. Takada visited Professor Takahashi, an acquaintance of Mr. Lerner's. It was the first time that Mr. Takada had met Professor Takahashi, and he spoke to him very politely. When they were leaving, he said

> *Doomo ojikan-o torimashite. . .*
> どうも　お時間を　とりまして……
> (I'm very sorry to have taken your time.)

and Professor Takahashi said

> *Iie, ohikitome-shimashite. . .*
> いいえ、おひきとめしまして……

which literally means "I kept you too long and I'm sorry for that." The professor, however, had not tried to detain them when they expressed their desire to leave, and Mr. Lerner wondered if this were another one of the set expressions said by a host to his visitors.

*　　*　　*

In polite conversation, a visitor usually apologizes for taking the host's time when leaving, as in

> *Ojama-shimashita.*
> (I'm sorry to have disturbed you.)

or

> *Ojikan-o torimashite. . .*

And the host will apologize for his not having entertained the visitor more, as in

Nanimo okamai-dekimasen-de. . .
(I'm sorry I couldn't do anything to entertain you.)

Or, he will sometimes apologize for taking the visitor's time by keeping him, as in *Ohikitome-shimashite. . .* whether or not he has actually verbally asked the visitor to stay longer.

Also, in polite conversation one does not express his happiness over having a good time as freely as in familiar conversation, in which one will often say something like

Kyoo-wa tanoshikatta-wane.
(We had a lovely time, didn't we?)
Jitsu-ni yukai-datta-ne.
(We had a great time, didn't we?)

Some foreigners like to express their pleasure in polite conversations too, as in

Kyoo-wa hontoo-ni tanoshikatta-desu.
(I had a very good time today.)

Although the Japanese do not usually use this expression themselves, they will understand that it is well-meant.

31

Joozu-desu-ne
じょうずですね
(You do it very well)

Mr. Lerner and Miss Yoshida were invited to Professor Takahashi's last Saturday. When they came into the room, Miss Yoshida noticed that there was a new picture hanging on the wall, and said

Joozuna e-desu-ne.
じょうずな　絵ですね。
(It's a well-done picture.)

But when Professor Takahashi said that he had painted the picture himself, Miss Yoshida blushed and hurriedly said *Shitsuree-shimashita* (Excuse me). Mr. Lerner wondered why she apologized for her praise; is it against etiquette to praise a picture done by one's superior?

*　　　*　　　*

It is usual for people to say nice things to others in social situations; a visitor will compliment the host on his house or family members. It is common to say such things as

Ii osumai-desu-ne.
(You have a very nice home.)
Kawaii okosan-desu-ne.
(She is a lovely child.)

But the Japanese usually refrain from directly praising someone's ability or skill in social situations. Since the word *joozu* means "skillful," it is not appropriate to use it to refer to someone with whom you have to be polite.

In the case above, Miss Yoshida probably thought that the picture had been painted by a younger relative, possibly a niece or grand-daughter, when she used the word *joozu*. It is all right for an adult to use this word to a child, or when you are talking in a familiar way, but when talking politely, you should not say things like

*Joozu-desu-ne.*1
(You do it very well)
or
Joozu-ni dekimashita.
(You did it very well.)

If Miss Yoshida had known who had painted the picture, she would have used some other expression such as

Kiree-desu-ne.
きれいですね。
(How beautiful!)
Suteki-desu-ne.
すてきですね。
(How nice!)
Subarashii e-desu-ne.
すばらしい 絵ですね。
(It's a wonderful picture.)

Naorimashita
なおりました
(It has been repaired)

Mr. Lerner took his cassette tape recorder to an electric appliance store the other day to have it fixed. He went back to the store today and asked for it, saying

Naoshimashita-ka.
(Have you repaired it?)

Then the clerk said, while bringing his recorder

Hai, naorimashita.
はい、なおりました。
(Yes, it has been repaired.)

Mr. Lerner wondered if *Naoshimashita* was wrong. He remembered that when he had said *Kaze-o naoshimashita* (*lit.* I cured my cold) a few days before, Miss Yoshida had corrected it to *Kaze-ga naorimashita* (*lit.* My cold has been cured.)

*　　　*　　　*

When referring to curing some sickness, the word *naoru* (to be recovered) is usually used rather than *naosu* (to cure) whether or not one has tried to cure it. *Naosu* is used only when one wants to emphasize one's own strong will to cure a sickness, as in

Byooki-o naosu koto-ga ichiban taisetsu-desu.
(The most important thing is to try to cure your illness.)

Since *naosu* implies a strong will or effort, the clerk at the electric appliance store avoided using it; if he had said

Hai, naoshimashita.

that would have sounded boastful and inappropriate.

When one refers to a service he has performed for the listener, it is polite to describe the action as if it has been done without special effort. For instance, when serving tea, it sounds more modest to say

Ocha-ga hairimashita.
お茶が　入りました。

(Tea is ready — *lit.* Tea has been poured.)
than
Ocha-o iremashita.

(I made tea.)

Sometimes the Japanese choose completely different expressions to avoid using a verb that directly describes their actions. For instance, when someone has written a letter of recommendation, he may say

Moo dekite-imasu-yo.
もう　できていますよ。

(It's ready now.)

Sore-ga. . .
それが……
(That. . .)

Mr. Lerner and Mr. Takada were talking before work yesterday morning, when Miss Yoshida came in. Mr. Takada asked her *Otooto-san, doo-datta?* (How did your brother do?), obviously referring to the results of a college entrance examination. Then Miss Yoshida just said

> *Sore-ga. . .*
> それが……
> (That. . .)

and Mr. Takada immediately said

> *Aa, dame-datta-no.*
> (Oh, he didn't make it.)

Mr. Lerner wondered how such a short phrase as *Sore-ga* was enough to answer a question.

*   *   *

Sore-ga. . . (*lit.* That. . .) is used to indicate that the answer is contrary to the listener's expectation, as in

A: *Ano eega omoshirokatta-deshoo.*
  (You enjoyed that movie very much, didn't you?)
B: *Sore-ga-nee. . .*
  (Well, that was. . .)
A: *Tsumaranakatta-no.*
  (It was boring?)
B: *Ee.*
  (Yes.)

You can either stop after *sore-ga* as in B's speech above, or complete the sentence as in

   B:*Sore-ga zenzen omoshiroku nakatta-n-desu.*
   (It was not at all interesting.)
or
   B:*Sore-ga omoshiroi dokoro-ka taikutsu-de nemuku natchaimashita.*
   (Far from being interesting, it was so dull that I became sleepy.)

In the case above, Mr. Takada's question sounded as if he was expecting to hear good news from Miss Yoshida, so she used this expression to indicate that she had bad news instead. If the question is asked without any expectation, some other expression will be used.

Sometimes *sore-ga. . .* is used to signify that the speaker's own expectation has been betrayed, as in

   Totemo ukaranai-to omoimashita. Sore-ga ukatta-n-desu.
   (I thought I could never pass the exam, but unexpectedly I passed it!)

This use of *sore-ga* sounds rather dramatic; you might use *demo* (but) or *keredomo* (but) instead if you don't want to emphasize the unexpectedness.

Kekkon-shite-imasu
結婚しています
(She's married)

Yesterday afternoon Miss Kawaguchi, one of his colleagues, came to see Mr. Lerner and asked him to attend her wedding, which was going to be held quite soon. When she was about to leave, Mr. Takada came in, so Mr. Lerner told him

Kawaguchi-san-wa kekkon-shite-imasu.
川口さんは　結婚しています。

meaning "Miss Kawaguchi is getting married." To his surprise, she blushed and hurriedly denied it by saying

Sonna koto, arimasen.
そんなこと、ありません。
(That's not so, *lit.* There's no such thing!)

*　　　*　　　*

The . . .*te-imasu* form is used in several ways. One of the most common uses is to indicate that an action is being performed, as in

Ima ocha-o nonde-imasu.
(I'm having tea now.)
Nani-o kangaete-imasu-ka.
(What are you thinking?)

Another common use of the . . .*te-imasu* form is to indicate a state of being, as in

Kekkon-shite-imasu.
(I'm married.)
Yasuku natte-imasu.

(It has become less expensive.)

With verbs that indicate completion of an action
or change of state, the . . .*te-imasu* form means
that the action has been completed and a certain
state of being has resulted. For instance, *kekkon-
shite-imasu* means that the person has gotten
married and is married now, and *yasuku natte-
imasu* means a thing has become, and is now,
less expensive. On the other hand, when used
with verbs that describe a state or an action
which usually continues for some time, the . . .*te-
imasu* indicates an action that is taking place
now, as in *nonde-imasu* (I'm drinking it) or *kan-
gaete-imasu* (I'm thinking).

The . . .*te-imasu* form is not, however, used
to refer to a future action unless a definite time
is indicated. Namely, you can say things like

Rainen-no imagoro-wa kekkon-shite-imasu.
(I'll be married about this time next year.)

But you cannot use . . .*te-imasu* to indicate a future action at an indefinite time. If you say just
kekkon-shite-imasu, it means that someone is married; it cannot mean that the person is getting
married.

Iku-n-da-tte?
行くんだって？
(Did you say he's going?)

When Mr. Lerner came back to the office from lunch yesterday, his colleagues were talking about their plan for flower-viewing. Mr. Takada asked Miss Yoshida

Iku-n-da-tte?
行くんだって？

and she answered

Ee, iku-n-da-tte.
ええ、行くんだって。

Mr. Lerner thought this exchange meant "Did you say you're going?" "Yes, I said I'm going." But all of a sudden Miss Yoshida turned to him and said

Ne, soo-deshoo?
(Right, Mr. Lerner?)

He realized then that they had been talking about him, but couldn't help wondering how he could have known who the subject of the sentence was in such a case as this. He had learned that -tte stands for -to, but couldn't Miss Yoshida have meant "I said I am going."?

* * *

. . . tte is used in place of . . . to, as in

Ashita-wa ame-da-tte iimashita.
(They said it will rain tomorrow.)

40

Iku-tte yakusoku-shimashita.
(I promised that I would go.)

But when the sentence ends with . . . *tte,* it is limited to the case when the speaker conveys what someone else said. In other words, . . . *tte* can mean either "you said" or "he/she/they said," but it cannot mean "I/We said." Therefore when Miss Yoshida said *Iku-n-da-tte,* she could not have meant "I said I am going"; it was obvious that she was referring to someone else.

If Mr. Takada and Miss Yoshida had been talking about her intentions, it would have been:

Mr. Takada: *Iku-n-da-tte?* (Did you say you're going?)

Miss Yoshida: *Ee, iku-wa.* (Yes, I'm going.)
or
Ee, iku-tte itta-wa. (Yes, I said I'm going.)

Thus . . . *tte* used at the end of a sentence is quite similar to . . . *soo-desu,* as in

Ashita-wa ame-da-soo-desu.
(I hear it will rain tomorrow.)

The difference between . . . *tte* and . . . *soo-desu* is that the former sounds more familiar.

Soo-desu-yone
そうですよね
(That's certainly so, isn't it?)

When Mr. Lerner was talking with his colleagues at lunchtime yesterday, Mr. Takada said something about the generation gap in Japan, and asked Mr. Lerner's opinion. Mr. Lerner completely agreed with him, so he said

Soo-desu-ne.
(That's right, isn't it?)

and then added *yo* for emphasis. But his colleagues said that *yo* sounds strange when added to *ne*. They said that they say *Soo-desu-yone* but never say *Soo-desu-neyo*.

Mr. Lerner had been trying to use *ne* and *yo* correctly; just recently he had found out that the two particles can be used together, but he had not learned that there is a fixed order for them.

* * *

As is generally explained, *ne* is used to solicit the listener's agreement and *yo* is used to emphatically express one's opinion. Thus *ne* can be paraphrased as "I hope you agree" or "don't you agree?" and *yo* as "I tell you" or "I assure you." They are usually used by themselves, but sometimes used together as in *Soo-desu-yone* or

Moo jikan-desu-yone.
もう　時間ですよね。
(*lit*. It's time now, I tell you — don't you agree?)

Ii hito-desu-yone.
(He's certainly a nice person, don't you

42

think?)

In such use, the order of *yo* and *ne* cannot be reversed; *ne* always comes last. When one says . . . *yone*, he is first expressing his opinion emphatically, and then turning to the listener for agreement.

In addition to *yo*, *ne* is used with other particles such as *no* or *wa*, always coming after them; sometimes it comes after two other particles as in

Sonna koto-wa nai-no-yo-ne.
そんなことはないのよね。
(*lit*. That's certainly not so, don't you agree?)

Mada osoku nai-wa-yo-ne.
(It's surely not too late, don't you agree?)

Compared with using just *yo*, *wa* or *no* alone, adding *ne* to such particles serves to express the speaker's concern toward the listener more precisely and more delicately.

Kekkon-suru soo-desu
結婚する そうです
(I hear she's getting married)

Mr. Lerner heard that Miss Kawaguchi, one of his colleagues, is getting married. He wondered what the Japanese expression for "She's getting married" was, and carried out a small experiment. He asked several colleagues if they had heard the news about her. Then Mr. Kobayashi, the youngest worker, said

Ee, kekkon-suru soo-desu-ne.
ええ、結婚する そうですね。
(Yes, I heard that she's getting married.)

Mr. Mori, the director of the company, said

Un, kekkon-suru-n-da-tte-ne.
うん、結婚するんだってね。
(Yes, I heard she's getting married. — more familiar than Mr. Kobayashi's expression)

And Miss Yoshida said

Ee, kekkon-nasaru-n-desu-tte-ne.
ええ、結婚なさるんですってね。
(Yes, I heard she's getting married. — more polite and feminine)

Mr. Lerner noticed that none of them used any special expression to indicate the future. He wondered if *kekkon-shimasu* or *kekkon-suru* means "she will get married" rather than "she gets married."

*　　　*　　　*

The dictionary form of a verb or the *-masu* form is usually used to indicate what is going to take place in the future, as in

Ashita-wa dekakeru-yo.
(I'll go out tomorrow.)
Rainen kaette-kimasu.
(I'll return next year.)

When necessary, phrases to indicate specific time in the future such as *rainen, ashita,* etc., are used. If one wants to emphasize that the action will take place immediately, one uses such expressions as *sugu* (immediately) and *kore-kara* (from now).

The expression . . . *te-imasu* (be . . .ing) is not, however, used to indicate a future action. *Dekakete-imasu* means "He's out"; you have to say

Dekakemasu.

to mean "I'm going out" or "I'll go out."

Osoku narimashite . . .
おそく　なりまして……
(I'm sorry I'm late)

Mr. Okada came to discuss some business with Mr. Lerner and Mr. Takada yesterday afternoon. When he entered the room he said

Osoku narimashite . . .
おそく　なりまして……
(I'm sorry I'm late.)

as he often does, although he was just a few minutes late. Then when they started their discussion Mr. Takada said

Daitai-no an-ga dekimashite . . .
だいたいの　案が　できまして……
(We have made a rough plan.)

Mr. Lerner noticed that both of these sentences were not completed; he remembered that the Japanese very often end their sentences with just . . . *mashite* rather than . . . *mashita.*

* * *

In terms of grammar, the . . . *te* form indicates continuation and corresponds to ". . . and," as in

Asa okite kao-o aratte shokuji-o shimashita.

(I got up, washed my face, and had breakfast.)

But in actual conversation the Japanese very often end their sentences with just . . . *te* or . . . *mashite.* There are several uses of this. In one use people often leave out what can be easily understood in set expressions of thanks or apology.

In another use, the speaker invites the listener to complete a sentence that is left unfinished. For instance, saying *Daitai-no an-ga dekimashite . . .* (*lit*. A rough plan has been made and . . .) invites the listener to say something like *Moo sukoshi-desu-ne* (That leaves just a little to be done, doesn't it?). It is regarded as good in Japanese conversation for two people, the speaker and listener, to participate in completing one statement. This is also related to the use of *aizuchi*, short reply words. You will find numerous examples of this use of the *. . . te* form in listening to how the Japanese talk. Just this morning your Japanese neighbors must have been talking like this:

A: *Kyoo-wa kaze-mo nakute . . .*
   (There is no wind today, and . . .)
B: *Ii otenki-desu-ne.*
   (It's a nice day, isn't it?)

47

Kore, tsutsunde
これ つつんで
(Wrap this, will you?)

Mr. Lerner bought a shirt at a department store near his office yesterday afternoon. The clerk took his money saying

Shooshoo omachi-kudasai.
(Would you please wait a moment?)

Then he handed the shirt to a young girl standing near him, saying

Kore, tsutsunde.
これ、つつんで。
(Wrap this, will you?)

Mr. Lerner understood that this was a command and imagined that it must be the abbreviation of *Tsutsunde-kudasai.* He wondered if this form is used only to those below one in age or position.

*　　　*　　　*

There are various expressions used for making a request or giving an instruction. The most common expressions are:

. . . *kudasai,* as in
Kaite-kudasai. (Please write it.)
. . . *kudasaimasen-ka,* as in
Kaite-kudasaimasen-ka. (Won't you please write it?)

And in familiar conversation male speakers often use

. . . *kure,* as in *Kaite-kure.* (Write it.)

The form ending with . . . *te* as in *Kore, tsu-tsunde* is used very often in familiar conversation. The clerk above used it toward his subordinate, and a parent will say to a child something like

To-o shimete. (Close the door, will you?)

It is also used between equals in familiar conversation, especially by female speakers, and sometimes even toward one's superiors when there is no need to be polite.

In case of emergency one often chooses this form rather than saying . . . *te-kudasai* or . . . *te-kudasaimasen-ka.* For example, an elderly wife who usually speaks politely to her husband may say when she is holding a shelf that is about to fall,

Otoosan, chotto kite!
お父さん、ちょっと 来て！

(Come and help, dear!)

Or, when people are engaged in an activity which requires unity, politeness is often replaced by an emphasis on togetherness. For instance, when faculty members and the new students of a college sit together for a photograph, the photographer will usually say to the group

Hai, waratte!
はい、笑って！

(Smile, everybody!)

rather than *Waratte-kudasai,* even if distinguished professors are included in the group.

Sonna koto arimasen-tara
そんな こと ありませんたら
(That's not so!)

Mr. Kato teased Miss Yoshida as usual for looking very nice and wondered if she wasn't getting married soon. Miss Yoshida said, as if tired of his teasing,

> *Sonna koto arimasen-tara.*
> そんな こと ありませんたら。

Mr. Lerner understood that she meant Mr. Kato was wrong, but wondered about the *tara* at the end of her sentence. Does this mean "If" as in *jikan-ga attara* (if there is time)?

*   *   *

. . . *arimasen-tara* is the abbreviation of . . . *arimasen-to ittara* (if I say there isn't . . .): Miss Yoshida's sentence above can be paraphrased as:

> *Sonna koto-wa arimasen-to ittara, arimasen.*
> (*lit.* If I say there is no such thing, there is no such thing.)

Actually this *tara* is added to a sentence for emphasis rather than to mean "if." It usually indicates that the speaker is irritated or bored at having to repeat what he has already said.

A mother will say to a child who will not get up even though she has called him several times,

> *Okinasai-ttara!*
> 起きなさいったら！
> (Get up!)

Or, a man will say to his friend who persistently asks him to go drinking together,

> *Dame-da-ttara!*
> だめだったら！
> (No, I can't!)

. . . *tara*, or often . . . *ttara*, is used in this way in familiar conversation by both men and women. It can be added either to polite sentences as in *arimasen-tara* or plain sentences as in *naittara*; the former is used only by women. When *tara* is used in this way, it is said with a falling tone.

This is different from the use of *tara* for making a suggestion, which is said with a rising tone as in:

> *Moo okitara?*
> (Why don't you get up now?)
> *Nanika tabete-ittara?*
> (Why don't you eat something before you go?)

51

Sumimasen, osoku natte
すみません、おそく　なって
(I'm sorry to be late)

Mr. Lerner and Mr. Takada asked Miss Yo-shida to go drinking with them after work last Friday. The two men left the office earlier and waited for her. She kept them waiting for several minutes, and then came out hurriedly. She said

Sumimasen, osoku natte.
すみません、おそく　なって。
(I'm sorry to be late.)

and the three started walking. There was nothing strange about it, but Mr. Lerner wondered why Miss Yoshida had reversed the order of the two phrases: is there any difference between *Sumima-sen, osoku natte* and *Osoku natte sumimasen*?

      *   *   *

In Japanese textbooks several common expressions of apology are given, as in:

Osoku natte sumimasen.
Omataseshite mooshiwake arimasen.
(I'm sorry to have kept you waiting — po-lite.)
Machigaechatte gomen-nasai.
(I'm sorry I made a mistake — familiar.)

But in actual conversation the order is very often reversed, and saying *sumimasen* or *gomen-nasai* first is very common. Not only in expres-sions of apology but also in various other expres-sions, phrases ending with . . . *te* are very often said later when they indicate the reason or basis for judgment. For instance,

Ii tokoro-desu-yo, midori-ga ookute.
(It's a nice place with lots of green leaves.)
Komarimashita-yo, okane-ga tarinakute.
(We had a difficult time because we didn't
have enough money.)
Iyada-naa, mata ame-ga futte.
(How annoying, it's raining again.)

This reversed order gives the impression that
the speaker is anxious to express his feelings.
Saying *Sumimasen, osoku natte* is appropriate
when the speaker has hurried and is out of
breath. In other words, saying things in this order sounds more emotional than otherwise and it
is more appropriate in familiar conversation
where formality is not required.

Irasshaimase
いらっしゃいませ
(I'm glad you have come)

After business discussions the other day, Mr. Okada took Mr. Lerner and Mr. Takada to a Japanese restaurant for dinner. When they entered the restaurant, several employees called out loudly

Irasshaimase!
いらっしゃいませ。
(Thank you for coming.)

Mr. Lerner answered *Konban-wa* (Good evening), but the other two men said nothing. This had happened several times before, but Mr. Lerner still felt uneasy about how he should act in such a situation.

*   *   *

To greet their customers, store clerks and restaurant employees say *Irasshaimase* or *Irasshai* (less formal); they do not say *Konnichi-wa* (Good day) or *Konban-wa* unless the customer is a personal acquaintance. In other words, there is a distinction between those who serve and those who are served in the style of greetings, and customers do not usually reply to *Irasshaimase* or *Irasshai*. Some customers answer by saying *Konnichi-wa* or *Konban-wa* or *Doomo* (Hi), but one is not required to do so.

The expression *Irasshaimase,* or *Irasshai,* literally means "Please come in," and actually corresponds to "I'm glad you have come." The ending *mase* indicates a very polite request; it can also be added to other expressions such as *Okaeri-*

nasai (*lit.* Welcome home), *Oagari-kudasai* (Please come in — *lit.* Please come up), and *Itte-irasshai* (*lit.* Please go and come home; used to see someone off). Expressions with *mase* sound very polite and nowadays people do not use them very often except for greeting customers.

The less formal version, *Irasshai,* is sometimes used between friends, especially women, and toward younger people. Women often say to their friends *Irasshai* or *Ara, irasshai* (Oh, it's you! How nice to see you). A teacher may say *Irasshai* to a student who has come to visit him at home.

Irasshai or *Irasshaimase* is different from *Irasshaimashita,* which literally means "someone has come"; you have to add *yoku* and say *Yoku irasshaimashita* (*lit.* It's good that you have come) to welcome someone.

Ashi-o fumaremashita
足を ふまれました
(Someone stepped on my foot)

Mr. Lerner had to take an especially crowded train to the office yesterday morning. When he arrived at the office, he was tired and was resting a while before starting his work. Miss Yoshida asked him if he was all right, so he explained that the train had been crowded, and added

Dareka-ga ashi-o fumimashita.
(Someone stepped on my foot.)

Then he remembered that the passive form is more appropriate and said

Ashi-ga fumaremashita.
(My foot was stepped on.)

Miss Yoshida immediately understood but said he should have said

Ashi-o fumaremashita.
足を ふまれました。

instead.

* * *

In conversational Japanese the passive form is used to indicate that someone has been affected by the action of someone else as in

(Watashi-wa) kachoo-ni shikararemashita.
(I was scolded by the section chief.)
(Watashi-wa) okane-o nusumaremashita.
(I had my money stolen.)

In the above sentences, *Watashi-wa* is left out when it can be understood from the situation, but in such passive sentences the subject must be the person who suffers from the action of someone else rather than the person's belongings. Therefore you can say either

    Watashi-wa ashi-o fumaremashita.
  or
    Ashi-o fumaremashita.

when someone has stepped on your foot, but it sounds strange to say

    Ashi-ga fumaremashita.
    (My foot was stepped on.)

In the same way, when you have had to pay taxes against your will, you will say

    Zeekin-o torareta.
    (*lit.* I had my taxes taken.)

rather than

    Zeekin-ga torareta.
    (*lit.* My taxes were taken.)

Sen-en-ni narimasu
千円に　なります
(That will be ¥1,000)

Mr. Lerner bought a cigarette lighter at a department store the other day. When he was ready to pay, the salesgirl looked at the price tag and said

> *Sen-en-ni narimasu.*
> 千円に　なります。
> (That will come to ¥1,000.)

Mr. Lerner paid her, took the lighter, and left the store. While doing so, he wondered why the girl had said . . . *ni narimasu* when he had bought just one lighter. If he had bought more than one article, the girl would have had to add up the sum, and in that case it would have been quite reasonable to say *Sen-en-ni narimasu*. He wondered if . . . *ni narimasu* is nothing more than a synonym for . . . *desu.*

*　　　*　　　*

. . . *ni narimasu* by itself means "something becomes. . ." or "something comes up to. . ." It is used to indicate change as in

> *Ashita-wa ame-ni narimasu-yo.*
> (It will rain tomorrow — *lit.* Tomorrow will become rainy.)

Or, one says when giving the total sum

> *Zenbu-de ichiman-en-ni narimasu.*
> (It comes to ¥10,000 in all.)

In actual conversation, however, . . . *ni narimasu* is often used even when there is no change or adding involved, as in Mr. Lerner's experience mentioned above. You can take this use of . . . *ni narimasu* as a synonym for . . . *desu* as far as the meaning is concerned. The difference between the two expressions is in the attitude of the speaker. The speaker usually chooses . . . *ni narimasu* when trying to be polite; . . . *desu* is more direct and consequently can sound abrupt. Saying *Sen-en-ni narimasu* can imply that the right procedure, such as adding up all costs, has been taken before deciding on a reasonable price. But in most cases the speaker uses this expression simply because it sounds more indirect and polite than . . . *desu*. This use of . . . *ni narimasu* is often preferred by clerks when talking to their customers. A clerk may say to a customer who has asked for a less expensive umbrella,

Motto oyasuino-deshitara, kochira-no aoino-ni narimasu.
もっと　お安いのでしたら、こちらの　青いのに なります。
(If you would like a less expensive one, there is this blue one — *lit*. If it is a less expensive one, it comes to this blue one.)

Soo-kamo shiremasen
そうかも　しれません
(That may be so)

Mr. Lerner and Mr. Takada were talking with Mr. Okada after business discussions yesterday afternoon, when Mr. Okada started talking about his daughter, a college student. He said that she seemed to be suffering from an unhappy love, but she would not talk to him about it; he was afraid that a father could do very little for his daughter in such situations. Mr. Lerner felt he should not sound too ready to agree with him on this point and was wondering what to say, when Mr. Takada said

>*Soo-kamo shiremasen-ne.*
>そうかも　しれませんね。
>(That may be so.)

and turned the conversation to a different topic.

*　　*　　*

The expression . . . *kamo shiremasen* literally means "whether or not . . . is not known"; it is used when one does not know something for sure. For instance, when you ask someone about the weather, he may say

>*Ashita-wa ame-kamo shiremasen-ne.*
>(It may rain tomorrow.)

In social situations, however, one often uses . . . *kamo shiremasen* when one wants to express one's judgment with reserve. In a sense it can be used as an understated way of saying "yes, that's right." In Mr. Takada's case above, he could have agreed with Mr. Okada saying

> *Soo-desu-ne.* (That's right.)

or

> *Soo-deshoo-ne.* (That must be so.)

But he probably chose *Soo-kamo shiremasen* because he did not want to discourage Mr. Okada by sounding too ready to admit that a father is of little help.

In a similar way, when a woman asks her friend's opinion about a new dress she is trying on, her friend may say

> *Chotto hade-kamo shirenai-wane.*
> (It may be a little bit too bright for you.)

rather than frankly say that the dress is not becoming to her at all.

Shochuu omimai-mooshiagemasu
暑中　お見舞い申し上げます
(Summer Season Greetings)

When Mr. Takada mentioned that he had not yet made plans for the summer, Miss Yoshida said that it was about time for her to start preparing *shochuu-mimai*. Mr. Lerner didn't know the word, but when Miss Yoshida showed him several cards she had received last year, he remembered that he had received some himself. The card said

Shochuu omimai-mooshiagemasu.
暑中　お見舞い申し上げます。
(*lit.* I am inquiring after your health in this hot season.)

He liked the idea of sending this type of cards, but wondered why the Japanese do not send such cards in the winter; is the winter easier to cope with than the summer in Japan?

＊　　　＊　　　＊

The word *mimai* or *omimai* means "visiting someone or sending a card to someone to inquire how he is." One does this most often for a sick person or a person who is suffering from a serious loss. *Shochuu-mimai,* or more correctly *Shochuu-mimaijoo* (*joo* means a "card"). is sent in the middle of summer just as one sends a card of best wishes for the New Year on the first of January. You might think of it as the summer version of "season's greeting." Since the New Year's card takes care of the winter, there is no need of sending *mimai* in the winter.

Many Japanese regard highly sending cards

regularly every year, and also sending cards at each point of important change in their life. For instance, many Japanese send cards, often printed, when they change their work, address, or marital status. Many Japanese think it most important to send cards when they change their position or work. We have heard some Japanese complain that their foreign acquaintances often leave Japan without any notice, using the phrase

aisatsu-mo shinaide . . .
  (without due greetings)

Dropping just a line to say that you are leaving Japan and thanking them for the kindnesses you have received during your stay will please your Japanese acquaintances more than you might think.

Moo yameru-n-da
もう やめるんだ
(Now stop it)

Mr. Lerner visited the Takadas last Saturday evening. After dinner he was talking with Mr. and Mrs. Takada when their youngest son, about five years old, came and wanted to join them. Then Mr. Takada said

Kodomo-wa moo neru-n-da.
子供は　もう　寝るんだ。
(*lit.* Children now go to bed.)

Mr. Lerner realized that sentences ending with . . . *n-da* are a kind of command, and remembered that Mr. Mori sometimes says

Shigoto-wa moo yameru-n-da.
仕事は　もう　やめるんだ。
(*lit.* As for work, you stop now.)

when he comes around to see his men on Friday evenings.

*　　*　　*

There are several expressions of command which are used depending on the situation. The form called "plain imperative," such as *ike* (go!) or *yamero* (stop!), is used mostly by men in familiar conversation, or in an urgent situation. Women seldom use this form to end a sentence.

The form ending with . . . *nasai* is used mainly by parents or schoolteachers toward children; except in set phrases such as *okaerinasai* (welcome home), one seldom uses it in social situations.

In social situations, one chooses a form of request rather than command, and . . . *te-kudasai* is most commonly used, as in *yamete-kudasai* (please stop it).

In familiar conversation such short forms as *yamete* or *yamete-ne* are used; women use them often, and men also use them when talking to younger people.

The form ending with . . . *n-da*, which is used for explanation or emphasis, is also used for giving command; *yameru-n-da* is not as blunt as *yamero* and not as polite as *yamete-kudasai*. Sometimes *da* is replaced by *desu* or *desu-yo* to make it sound softer. A nurse may say to a patient something like

> *Yukkuri yasumu-n-desu-yo.*
> (Now, take a long rest.)

even when the patient is older. This expression has a tone of explaining what the listener should do, and can sound patronizing.

Sometimes . . . *koto* is used in written notices as in

> *Rooka-wa hashiranai koto.*
> (No running in the hall.)

This is meant for students or employees; for customers more polite expressions like *hashiranaide-kudasai* (please do not run) must be used.

Itte-kurereba yokatta-noni
言ってくれれば　よかったのに
(You should have asked me)

Miss Yoshida said that her family had moved to a new house during the weekend. Mr. Lerner congratulated her and said it must have been a lot of work. He wanted to say that if she had told him about it he could have helped her, but he did not know how to say this. Then Mr. Takada said

Itte-kurereba yokatta-noni.
言ってくれれば　よかったのに。
(You should have told me — *lit.* If you had kindly told me, it would have been good, but . . .)

*　　　*　　　*

The expression . . . *eba yokatta-noni* means "although one should have done . . ." as in

Gofun hayaku okireba yokatta-noni.
(I should have gotten up five minutes earlier.)

which implies that the speaker actually overslept and was late.

When Mr. Takada said *Itte-kurereba yokatta-noni*, he implied that Miss Yoshida should have asked them to help her. The words, . . . *kurereba yokatta-noni* (if you had been kind enough to . . . it would have been better) would appear to criticize the listener, but actually express the speaker's willingness to help; therefore this is often used in social situations. To a visitor who has found his way by himself, the host may say

Denwa-shite-kudasareba yokatta-noni.
電話してくだされば　よかったのに。
(You should have called me.)

implying that he could have gone to the station or some place to meet him.

On more formal occasions, . . . *te-kurereba* (or . . . *te-kudasareba*) *yokatta-noni* is left out because it sounds as if it is criticizing the listener, even if this is not how the words are actually understood, and regret is expressed in the following way:

Omukae-ni agarimashita-noni . . . Doomo mooshiwake gozaimasen.
(I could have come to meet you. I'm very sorry I didn't.)

Maido arigatoo-gozaimasu
毎度　ありがとうございます
(Thank you very much for your patronage)

Mr. Lerner dined at a small restaurant near his office with Mr. Takada the other day. When they had paid and were about to leave, the clerk said,

Maido arigatoo-gozaimasu.
毎度　ありがとうございます。
(Thank you for your constant patronage —*lit.* Thank you every time.)

Mr. Lerner had never been there before, so he guessed that the clerk said *maido* (every time) because Mr. Takada often dined there. But later he found that Mr. Takada had never been there before either. Is it just customary to say *Maido arigatoo-gozaimasu,* even to a new customer?

*　　　*　　　*

The expression *Maido arigatoo-gozaimasu* literally means that the speaker is thanking someone who comes and does him a favor regularly. But even when the customer is new, the storekeeper or clerk often uses this expression; he is, whether consciously or not, trying to sound as if he is talking to someone who comes often. Many people think that it is more polite to treat someone as an old acquaintance than as a new visitor, and consequently use *maido* even to a newcomer.

The same idea is in operation when a barber or hairdresser says to a customer

Kyoo-wa donna fuu-ni shimashoo-ka.

(How would you like your hair done today?)

as if the customer had come before. Or, some-times a barber will say

> *Itsumo-no yoo-de yoroshii-desu-ka.*
> (Will the usual style do?)

even to a customer who has come for the first time.

In the case of a haircut, the barber can see what he should do by looking at the customer's present hairstyle, but in other cases it is impossible to know the customer's taste or wishes if he has not come before. A student of ours once made a small experiment; he went into a *sushi* shop where he had never been before, sat down at the counter, and said

> *Itsumo-no yatsu, tanomimasu.*
> (Give me the usual ones, please.)

Surprisingly enough, the *sushi* cook nodded and made several pieces of *sushi*, most of which were exactly what he wanted to have.

Zuibun
ずいぶん
(Terribly)

Mr. Lerner now wants to enlarge his vocabulary in Japanese, and has started using various words to mean "very." He realized that he has been using *taihen* all the time and that the Japanese seem to use various other words. Just today Miss Yoshida said to him

Raanaa-san-no nihongo, kono-goro zuibun umaku narimashita-ne.
ラーナーさんの　日本語、このごろ　ずいぶん
うまく　なりましたね。

(Your Japanese has been tremendously improved these days.)

He was very pleased to hear this, and replied

Zuibun arigatoo-gozaimasu.

to mean "Thank you very much." Miss Yoshida laughed and said it was a good joke, but Mr. Lerner wondered if *zuibun* can never be used with *arigatoo*.

*　　　*　　　*

Zuibun sounds familiar and cannot be used for formally expressing gratitude. It is an emotional expression in that it implies that the speaker is deeply impressed or affected by something. For instance, one will say

Yuube-wa zuibun furimashita-ne.
ゆうべは　ずいぶん　降りましたね。
(It rained a lot last night.)

70

implying that one was surprised at the amount of rain or inconvenienced by it. It is easy to understand why one uses *zuibun* in

    Kono-goro zuibun bukka-ga agarimashita-ne.
    (Things have become very expensive these days.)

After a test students might say things like

  A: *Zuibun muzukashikatta-ne.*
    (It was very hard, wasn't it?)
  B: *Un, sensee zuibun hidoi-yone.*
    (Yes, the teacher is very hard on us, isn't he?)

    Miss Yoshida could have used *taihen* or *totemo* instead of *zuibun* when she praised Mr. Lerner's Japanese, but she probably chose *zuibun* because she wanted to emphasize that she was very much impressed by his progress.

Ki-ni suru koto-wa arimasen-yo
気に する ことは ありませんよ
(You don't have to worry about it)

Yesterday morning Miss Yoshida came to the office with a new hair style. Mr. Lerner and Mr. Takada complimented her on it, but she said that the hairdresser had made it too short, and kept touching her hair nervously. Mr. Lerner said that her hair looked fine and added

   Shinpai-shinaide-kudasai.

meaning "Don't worry." Then Mr. Takada agreed with him and said

   Ki-ni suru koto-wa nai-yo.
   気に する ことは ないよ。
   (You don't have to be bothered by it.)

Mr. Lerner wondered if *shinpai* was the wrong word in this situation.

                 *   *   *

Shinpai usually refers to a concern about something rather serious. One uses *shinpai* when a family member is sick or he has to take up a difficult task. In such cases others will express their sympathy or encourage him by saying things like

   Sore-wa goshinpai-deshoo.
   (You must be very concerned.)
   Shinpai-wa irimasen. Umaku ikimasu-yo.
   心配は いりません。うまく いきますよ。
   (You don't have to worry. You will do it fine.)

On the other hand *ki-ni suru* means that you are aware that something is not very important but you cannot get it out of your mind, as in

Taishita machigai-ja nai-n-desu-kara, ki-ni suru koto-wa arimasen-yo.

(It isn't a serious mistake, so you don't have to feel bad about it.)

Therefore in the case of Miss Yoshida's hair, Mr. Lerner should have used *ki-ni suru* instead of *shinpai-suru*. In most cases *ki-ni suru* and *shinpai-suru* cannot be used interchangeably. Saying *kami-o ki-ni shite-imasu* describes Miss Yoshida's case, and if you said *kami-o shinpai-shite-imasu*, it would sound as if she were worrying about whether her hair will grow gray or damaged.

The form . . . *ga ki-ni naru* is also used in a similar way to . . . *o ki-ni suru* as in

Ame-no oto-ga ki-ni natte, nemuremasen-deshita.

(The sound of the rain got on my nerves and I couldn't sleep.)

Nemukute, nemukute. . .
ねむくて、ねむくて……
(I'm so sleepy)

Mr. Takada said that he had taken his family to visit his relatives in the country and had just come back the previous night. He looked very tired and while pouring coffee for himself, he said,

Kyoo-wa nemukute, nemukute. . .
今日は ねむくて、ねむくて……

Mr. Lerner said *Soo-desu-ka. Taihen-deshita-ne* (Is that right? It was tough, wasn't it?) just as an average Japanese would say to his colleague, but wondered what was left out after *nemukute. . .*

* * *

There are several expressions using a . . .*te* phrase for emphasizing one's feelings.

One is . . .*te tamaranai* as in

Samukute tamarimasen.
寒くて たまりません。

(It's unbearably cold—*lit.* I'm cold and can't stand it.)

Nemukute tamaranai-kara koohii-o nonde-imasu.

(I'm so sleepy that I'm drinking some coffee.—*lit.* I'm sleepy and can't stand it so I'm drinking coffee.)

Another is . . .*te shikata-ga nai* as in

Yametakute shikata-ga nai.

(I really want to quit—*lit*. I want to quit and there is nothing I can do about it.)

. . .*te shiyoo-ga nai* is also used as in

Hara-ga tatte shiyoo-ga arimasen.
(I'm just so angry—*lit*. I'm angry and I can do nothing about it.)

The last part of these expressions is added for emphasis and can be left out without making the sentence ambiguous. Mr. Takada said *Nemukute nemukute. . .* to mean that he was very sleepy, and the rest of the sentence can be any one of the phrases *tamaranai, shikata-ga nai* or *shiyoo-ga nai.* And to double the emphasis, he repeated the phrases *nemukute.*

The first part of the sentence takes the . . .*te* form, and it must be an expression of the speaker's own feelings. Usually adjectives are used as in

Ureshikute, ureshikute. . . (I'm so happy.)
Okashikute okashikute. . . (It's so funny.)
Sabishikute tamarimasen. (I'm so lonely.)

Sometimes verbs are used when they indicate the speaker's feelings.

Hara-ga tatte, hara-ga tatte. . . (I'm so angry.)
Sore-ga ki-ni natte shikata-ga arimasen.
(I'm very much bothered by that.)

Teeshoku-de ii-desu
定食で いいです
(Today's lunch will do)

Mr. Lerner had lunch at a Japanese restaurant near his office yesterday. The restaurant was crowded with office workers obviously from the neighborhood. Mr. Lerner had decided on the day's lunch and was going to say

Teeshoku-ni shimasu.

(I will take today's lunch — *lit*. I decide on the fixed lunch.)

when a young man sitting next to him said

Teeshoku-de ii-desu.
定食で いいです。
(Today's lunch will do.)

Mr. Lerner remembered that he had often heard people say . . . *de ii* when ordering a meal, and wondered if that is a fixed expression.

* * *

. . . *de ii* means " . . . will do" or " . . . is good enough although not the best" as in

Kyoo-wa ukagaemasen. Ashita-de ii-desu-ka.
(I can't come today. Will tomorrow do?)

When asking for something, many people like to use . . . *de ii* to express their reserve. They often ask someone to help them by saying

Ato-de ii-n-desu-kedo . . .
後で いいんですけど……

76

(You don't have to do it right away — *lit.* Later will do.)

When ordering a meal at a restaurant, too, customers will often say

    Sashimi-de ii. (*Sashimi* will do.)
    Nami-de ii-desu. (Regular (*sushi*) will do.)

instead of . . . *ni shimasu* or . . . *o kudasai,* implying that their order will be more convenient for those who prepare and serve the meals. By indicating that they are not demanding something just to satisfy their own need, they show consideration to the employees of the restaurant.

Sometimes . . . *de ii* is used to reflect the speaker's guilty feelings about ordering something not very lucrative for the restaurant. For instance, when five people come for lunch and order only two bottles of beer, they often say

    Nihon-de ii-n-da-kedo. (Two will do.)

implying that they are sorry not to order more.

Although many people are not conscious of these feelings behind . . . *de ii,* using that expression is regarded as more appropriate in such social situations than using simple and direct expressions like *Teeshoku-o kudasai* or *Teeshoku-ni shimasu.*

Boku-mo
ぼくも
(Me, too)

Mr. Lerner and Mr. Takada had some business discussions at Mr. Okada's office the other day. After the discussions, Mr. Okada took them to a nearby restaurant for lunch. Several of his colleagues went with them. When they had sat down and Mr. Lerner decided on *sashimi*, Mr. Takada said

Ja, boku-mo sashimi.
じゃ、ぼくも　さしみ。
(Then, I will have *sashimi*, too.)

Then Mr. Okada and his colleagues all said

Watashi-mo.
わたしも。
(Me, too.)

Mr. Lerner had noticed that Japanese people often order the same thing when they dine together, but it was the first time that he had seen five or six people all ask for the same thing.

* * *

It is true that Japanese often have the same meal even when it is possible to ask for different things. Sometimes they do this because they just feel lazy and do not want to think about what to order, but very often they do this because they feel they should.

When the members of a group know each other well enough not to have to pay special attention to each other, they usually order what they want. In other words, when they are in their own, well-established group, they do not have to conform to others. Family members, good friends or work colleagues usually fall into this category.

On the other hand, when they do not know each other that well and they have to try hard to establish good relations, they tend to order the same meal.

Sometimes when one of the people present wants to have something different for a special reason, he will add an explanation, as in

Watashi-wa udon-ni shimasu. Chotto i-no chooshi-ga warui-n-de.

(As for me, I will take noodles, since I am having some trouble with my stomach.)

when he feels that he should really order the same thing for the sake of better relations.

Koko-wa watashi-ga . . .
ここは わたしが……
(I will take care of this)

Mr. Lerner and Mr. Takada took Mr. Okada to a restaurant near their office after business discussions yesterday. After the meal, when Mr. Okada reached for the bill placed near Mr. Takada's plate, Mr. Takada said,

> *Koko-wa watashi-ga . . .*
> ここは わたしが……
> (*lit.* As for this place, I . . .)

obviously meaning "This is on me." Mr. Okada protested once and then accepted.

Mr. Lerner had learned the word *ogoru* (to treat) before, and wondered if one can also say

> *Watashi-ga ogorimasu.*
> (I'm going to treat you.)

in such a situation.

* * *

There are several expressions to mean that you are going to pay the bill for your guest. The word *ogoru* is informal and one can say

> *Kyoo-wa boku-ga ogoru.*
> (I'll treat you today.)

or

> *Watashi-no ogori-desu.*
> (It's my treat.)

only to good friends or to younger people.

Gochisoo-suru is also used to mean "to

treat," but this also is used by the person who pays only between good friends or when one does not have to be polite.

When you have to be polite, you should say

(Koko-wa) watashi-ga . . .

which is an abbreviation of *Koko-wa watashi-ga oharai-shimasu* (I'm going to pay this bill). In the same manner one also says

(Koko-wa) watashi-ni . . .
（ここは）　わたしに……

which is an abbreviation of *Koko-wa watashi-ni harawasete-kudasai* (Please let me pay this bill). In both cases *kyoo-wa* can replace *koko-wa*.

After *Koko-wa watashi-ga . . .* or *Koko-wa watashi-ni . . .* the verb is not mentioned. Words meaning "to pay" or "to treat" are often left out because people consider it impolite to mention them when they should be polite. To be even more polite, people sometimes slip out and pay the bill before the guest notices. When the guest realizes and asks to pay, the host will say,

Ie, kekkoo-desu.
(No, that's not necessary.)

Koko-ni kissaten-ga aru-desho?
ここに　喫茶店が　あるでしょ？
(There's a coffee shop here, you know?)

When Mr. Lerner and Miss Yoshida were talking during their break, Mr. Mori came up and
asked them how to get to the restaurant that they
had mentioned a few days before. Mr. Lerner
drew a rough sketch of the neighborhood and
started to explain. When he said, while pointing
to a spot on the paper,

> Koko-ni kissaten-ga aru-desho?
> ここに　喫茶店が　あるでしょ？
> (There's a coffee shop here, you know?)

Miss Yoshida said hurriedly

> Arimasu-ne?
> ありますね。
> (There is, isn't there?)

Mr. Lerner did not understand why she had done
this as if to correct his Japanese, but asked her
to finish the explanation. He listened to her as
she explained; she always said arimasu-ne and
never said aru-desho? although she had often
used this when talking with him.

*　　　*　　　*

The expression . . . deshoo is used to indicate probability, as in

> Yamada-san-nara dekiru-deshoo.
> (Mr. Yamada probably can do it.)
> Chikatetsu-ga ichiban hayai-deshoo.
> (I think the subway will probably be the fast-

est.)

Sometimes it is used as a polite substitute for
. . . *desu* as in

> *Donata-deshoo-da.* (May I ask who you are?)
> *Kore-deshoo-ka.* (Is this what you want?)

In informal conversation, . . . *deshoo* is
sometimes used with a rising tone to confirm the
listener's understanding, as in

> *Ashita-wa korareru-desho(o)?*
> (You can come tomorrow, right?)
> *Kore-de juubun-desho(o)?*
> (This is enough, don't you think?)

As it is informal, Mr. Lerner should not have
used it with Mr. Mori. He should have said *Kissaten-ga arimasu* or . . . *ga arimasu-ne* instead;
the former sounds more reserved.

This usage of *deshoo* is limited to conversation between good friends or speech toward
younger people. Women use it more often and
men often use *daroo?*, the less polite form instead. And this *deshoo* often is shortened to
desho?

Kimura-san-desu
木村さんです
(It's Mr. Kimura)

Mr. Lerner and Miss Yoṣhida were showing some pictures taken at the picnic in which several of the people from the office had participated the previous week. Mr. Mori particularly liked one of the pictures and asked them who had taken it. Miss Yoshida answered

> *Kimura-san-desu.*
> 木村さんです。
> (It's Mr. Kimura.)

Mr. Lerner wondered why she had said . . . *desu* when he would have said

> *Kimura-san-ga torimashita.*
> (Mr. Kimura did — *lit.* Mr. Kimura took it.)

*   *   *

Desu is often used when explaining or reporting what happened in the past as well as the present. In response to the question "Who took the picture?" the answer *Kimura-san-ga torimashita* is correct, but very often the answer is given with the . . . *desu* form as in

> *Kimura-san-desu.*

or

> *Watashi-desu.*

This type of answer will probably seem natural to a question that has been asked with the . . . *desu-ka* form as in

Kono shashin-o totta-nowa dare-desu-ka.

But an answer with . . . *desu* is also often given to a question that has not been asked with the . . . *desu-ka* form.

This is especially used when the person who answers is concerned more with a particular factor than with the fact as a whole. Even when the question is

Dare-ga kono shashin-o torimashita-ka.
(Who took this picture?)

one may say *Kimura-san-desu* rather than *Kimura-san-ga torimashita* if one's concern lies in the agent of the action rather than the fact that Kimura-san took a picture.

In the same way, one may answer

Hakone-desu. (*lit.* It's Hakone.)

to the question

Kinoo doko-e ikimashita-ka.
(Where did you go yesterday?)

just as to

Kinoo itta-nowa doko-desu-ka.
(What's the name of the place where you went yesterday?)

And this also applies to answers to questions in the present or in the future, as in

A: *Ginkoo-no mae-ni nani-ga arimasu-ka.*
   (What's in front of the bank?)
B: *Kissaten-desu.*
   (A coffee shop is.)

Kore, oishii-wane
これ、おいしいわね
(This is good, isn't it?)

Yesterday afternoon when Mr. Lerner and his colleagues were having tea, Miss Yoshida tasted a cookie and said

> Kore, oishii-wane. これ、おいしいわね。
> (This is good, isn't it?)

And Mr. Lerner agreed, saying inadvertently

> Soo. Oishii-wane.
> (Yes, it's good, isn't it?)

Then the colleagues all praised his Japanese; they obviously thought that Mr. Lerner had purposely used women's speech as a joke. He remembered then that men usually say *oishii-ne* instead of *oishii-wane,* but he was not sure how women's expressions are different from men's.

*　　　*　　　*

In familiar speech, men and women use sentence particles differently.

I. Verbs and adjectives:
    When the sentence ends with a verb or adjective, sentence particles are used as follows.

men	women
Ashita iku-yo.	Ashita iku-wayo.
	(I will certainly go tomorrow.)
Kore, ii-ne.	Kore, ii-wane.
	(This is good, isn't it?)

Kore, ii-yo.   *Kore, ii-wayo.*
                (This is certainly good.)

Namely, with verbs and adjectives women use *wa* before *yo* or *ne*.

II. Nouns and *na* adjectives:
In the case of sentences ending with a noun or an adjective with the *na* ending, sentence particles are used as follows.

men	women	
Ashita-dane.	*Ashita-ne.*	(It's tomorrow, isn't it?)
Soo-dane.	*Soo-ne.*	(It's so, isn't it?)
Shizuka-dayo.	*Shizuka-yo.*	(It certainly is quiet.)

In women's speech, . . . *da-wayo* and . . . *da-wane* are also used as more emphatic expression. But usually women avoid using *da* preceding a sentence particle.

In addition to the use of particles, the selection of vocabulary is different to some extent. Thus Japanese usually can tell whether a conversation is between men or women just by looking at a transcript. The following dialogues all say "It's good, isn't it?" "Yes, that's right." You might see if you can tell the sex of the speakers.

1. A: *Kore, oishii-wane.*   3. A: *Kore, oishii-ne.*
   B: *Un, soo-dane.*   B: *Ee, soo-ne.*
2. A: *Kore, oishii-wane.*   4. A: *Kore, umai-ne.*
   B: *Ee, soo-ne.*   B: *Un, soo-dane.*

The speakers are most likely: 1. woman and man; 2. woman and woman; 3. man and woman; 4. man and man.

Kore-wa are-deshoo-ne . . .
これは　あれでしょうね……
(This case is like that, isn't it?)

When Mr. Takada was explaining a new proposal to Mr. Mori, the director of the company, the other day, Mr. Mori asked him who would be best to help him in the project. Then Mr. Takada answered

> *Kore-wa are-deshoo-ne* . . .
> これは　あれでしょうね……
> (*lit.*This should be that, shouldn't it?)

and then named one of his colleagues. Mr. Lerner was interested in this expressions *are-deshoo-ne*. It seemed to him to have no substantive meaning; he wondered what function it serves.

*　　*　　*

Many Japanese regard it as important to sound hesitant or to give some kind of signal before expressing their opinion so that they will not sound abrupt. This is why they often use such phrases as *jitsu-wa* . . . (as a matter of fact), *anoo* . . . (well), *nan-to iimashoo-ka* (how should I put it?) before giving an opinion. *Are-deshoo-ne* is one such expression.

Are-deshoo-ne literally means "it is probably that, isn't it?" Its function is to indicate that the speaker expects the listener to agree with what he is going to say next.

When asking the listener's opinion, *doo-deshoo-ne* is used in a similar way; namely, it is said to indicate that the speaker is going to ask a question, as in

Kondo-no shiai-wa, doo-deshoo-ne, Kyojin-ga yappari tsuyoi-deshoo-ne.

(This match, what do you think, it will probably end in a Giants' victory, won't it?)

Deshoo is replaced by *daroo* when a male speaker is engaged in familiar conversation, as in

Kore, are-daroo-ne, ashita-made-niwa muri-daroo-ne.

これ、あれだろうね、あしたまでには 無理だろうね。

(You won't be able to finish this by tomorrow, will you?)

Gomen-kudasai
ごめんください
(Excuse me)

When Mr. Lerner was at home reading a magazine last Saturday, Mrs. Takahashi came to return a book that her husband had borrowed from him a few weeks before. She left without entering the house; when she was leaving, she said, while bowing,

Ja, gomen-kudasai.
じゃ、ごめんください。
(lit. Then, excuse me.)

Mr. Lerner understood that she meant "Good-bye," but he had thought that Gomen-kudasai is used only when calling someone to the door. Can the same expression be used both at the beginning and end of a visit?

*　　　*　　　*

Gomen-kudasai literally means "Please pardon me." It is usually used when a visitor calls out for someone to come to the door. And when the host or hostess comes to the door and asks the visitor to come in, the visitor will say

Shitsuree-shimasu.
失礼します。

while going into the house. Thus, Gomen-kudasai is used differently from Shitsuree-shimasu when used at the beginning of a visit.

When leaving, however, Gomen-kudasai as well as Shitsuree-shimasu can be used to mean "Good-bye." Both Gomen-kudasai and Shitsuree-

shimasu are more polite than *Sayoonara*. The difference between the two polite expressions is that *Gomen-kudasai* is used by older people, especially by older women.

Shitsuree-shimasu has a broader usage than *Gomen-kudasai* in that it can be used before taking any action that might be impolite. You can say *Shitsuree-shimasu* before picking up something, handing something over to someone, going into a room, temporarily leaving a person, and so on. *Gomen-kudasai* is not usually used in this way.

Desu-ne
ですね
(It is, isn't it?)

After business discussions yesterday afternoon Mr. Lerner and Mr. Takada took Mr. Okada to a nearby restaurant to have some beer. When Mr. Okada said

Shigoto-no ato-wa yappari biiru . . .
仕事の　あとは　やっぱり　ビール……
(The best thing to have after work is beer.)

Mr. Takada said

Desu-ne.
ですね。
(It is, isn't it?)

Mr. Lerner wondered if this was an abbreviation of *Soo-desu-ne*; if so, he thought he would use it often because it is so short.

*　　　*　　　*

In informal conversation one sometimes answers with just *Desu-ne* as Mr. Takada did. This is done usually when the speaker's sentence has not been completed. In this respect, this answer can be regarded as a kind of finishing up someone's statement. In fact, in Japanese conversation finishing up the speaker's unfinished sentence is regarded as a sign of positive participation, and it is natural for one person to leave part of his sentences unsaid and for the other person to finish them.

Several variations of *Desu-ne* are also used. For example, *Deshita-ne* is used as in:

A: *Kinoo ichiban saki-ni kita-nowa Yamamoto-san . . .*

B: *Deshita-ne.*

    (A: It was Mr. Yamamoto who came first yesterday. B: It was, wasn't it?)

And *Deshoo-ne* is used as in:

A: *Kore-ja chotto tarinai . . .*

    (A: This won't be sufficient. B: It won't, will it?)

    Answering with just *Desu-ne* or the like is limited to informal conversations. In a more formal situation Mr. Takada would have said *Soo-desu-ne* or *Hai, soo-desu-ne*. If the occasion is very formal one usually avoids using *ne* and says *Hai, soo-desu* or simply *Hai*. At that time, one also refrains from completing the speaker's statements and waits for him to finish them.

Mite-itadakemasen-ka
見ていただけませんか
(Would you please take a look at this?)

Mr. Lerner and Miss Yoshida planned a picnic for their colleagues and their families, and then conferred about it with Mr. Mori, the director of the company. After Miss Yoshida explained the plan, Mr. Lerner handed Mr. Mori the paper on which the details were written, saying

Kore, mite-kudasai.
(Please look at this.)

But Mr. Mori did not say anything for a moment. Mr. Lerner did not know what he had done to make him angry.

*   *   *

If Miss Yoshida had handed over the paper, she would have said

Chotto goran-itadakemasu-ka.
ちょっと　ごらんいただけますか。
(Would you please take a look at it?)
  or
Chotto mite-itadakemasen-ka.
ちょっと　見ていただけませんか。
(Would you please take a look at it?)

instead of saying *Mite-kudasai.*

The form . . . *te-kudasai* is appropriate in a classroom or business situation. But in situations where one has to be polite . . . *te-kudasai* is usually replaced by more polite expressions, such as . . . *te-itadakemasen-ka* or . . . *te-kudasaimasen-ka.*

The form . . . te-itadakemasen-ka as in

Kore, shirabete-itadakemasen-ka.
(Would you please check this?)
or
Kore, oshirabe-itadakemasen-ka.
(Would you please check this?)

is highly recommended as a polite expression for requests. A similar expression . . . te-kudasaimasen-ka is also polite, but it implies that the request is taken as a matter of course, which . . . te-itadakemasen-ka does not; therefore . . . te-itadakemasen-ka is more polite. Adding . . . deshoo-ka as in

Chotto shirabete-itadakemasen-deshoo-ka.

is very polite.

There are also some special words for showing respect such as *goran-ni naru* (see) and *meshiagaru* (eat), but if you add . . . te-itadakemasen-deshoo-ka or . . . te-itadakemasen-ka you can do without such words. You can use such expressions as

Mite-itadakemasen-deshoo-ka.
Nonde-itadakemasen-deshoo-ka.

any time you want to sound pleasant and polite.

Osokatta-desu-ne
おそかったですね
(You're late)

Mr. Lerner and several of his colleagues went on a picnic last Saturday. They met in front of a railway station in the morning, but Mr. Takada was late. When he finally showed up, Miss Yoshida said a little angrily

Osokatta-desu-ne.
おそかったですね。
(*lit.* You were late, weren't you?)

and Mr. Takada apologized. Mr. Lerner wondered why Miss Yoshida had used the past tense of *osoi*.

*   *   *

Both *osoi* and *osokatta* can be used to mean "You're late," but the speaker's attitude is different in the two cases. When one says *Osoi-desu-ne,* one is emphasizing the present state of the person being late, but when one says *Osokatta-desu-ne,* one is emphasizing the fact that a long time had elapsed before he came. In other words, the speaker is more concerned about what has preceded the present state of things than he is about the present state when he uses adjectives ending with . . . *ta.*

Sometimes both forms, the dictionary form and the . . . *ta* form, are used in similar situations. For instance, when thanking someone one sometimes says *Arigatoo-gozaimasu* and sometimes *Arigatoo-gozaimashita.* The latter is used when the speaker wants to emphasize that it has taken a considerable length of time or amount of trouble to complete the action. Thus *Arigatoo-gozaimashita* can be translated as "Thank you for "Thank you for having done so much for me."

Adjectives ending with . . . *ta* can also imply the speaker's psychological involvement in the process by which a certain state comes to an end. For instance, when hearing good news, saying *Yokatta-desu-ne* usually implies that the speaker has been concerned with the matter and is now released from that worry. Thus when you want to express your joy at hearing good news such as someone's having passed an important examination, it is more appropriate to say

> *Yokatta-desu-ne.*
> よかったですね。

than to say

> *Ii-desu-ne.*

Yasundara doo-desu-ka
休んだら　どうですか
(Why don't you rest?)

Mr. Takada was working very hard yesterday afternoon. When Miss Yoshida voluntarily made coffee for him and took it to him, he did not even look up. Miss Yoshida came to Mr. Lerner and said

> *Sukoshi yasumeba ii-noni.*
> (He should rest a little.)

Mr. Lerner agreed saying

> *Soo-desu-ne. Yasunda hoo-ga ii-desu-ne.*

to mean "That's right. He had better rest."
Then Miss Yoshida went to Mr. Takada again, and said

> *Sukoshi yasundara doo-desu-ka.*
> 少し　休んだら　どうですか。
> (Why don't you rest?)

Mr. Lerner realized that there are several expressions for giving advice, and wondered which of them is most common.

*   *   *

The three expressions . . . *eba ii-noni,* . . . *hoo-ga ii-desu* and . . . *tara doo-desu-ka* can all be used for giving advice.
The most common expression is . . . *tara doo-desu-ka* as in

> *Kochira-ni shitara doo-desu-ka.*

こちらに　したら　どうですか。

(Why don't you decide on this one?)

To make this expression more polite, you can change the wording as in

Kochira-ni nasattara ikaga-desu-ka.

And in informal speech one often says *doo?* instead of *doo-desu-ka.*

　. . . *hoo-ga ii-desu* is also used for giving advice as in

Hayaku kaetta hoo-ga ii-desu-yo.
(You had better go home early.)

This is usually said to one's equals or to younger people, since it implies that the speaker knows about the matter better than the other person.
　The expression . . . *eba ii-noni* literally means "If you did . . . , it would be better, but . . . " It implies criticism of the other person for what he is doing or has done; therefore it cannot be used in polite speech unless the advice is purely for the benefit of the other person. A host sometimes says to a visitor who has brought him a present

Konna koto shinakereba ii-noni.
(You shouldn't have done this.)
　or, more politely,
Konna koto nasaranakereba ii-nomi.

"Kono" to "Sono"
「この」と「その」
(This and that)

Mr. Lerner went to the barber yesterday evening. While waiting his turn, he listened to the conversation between the barber and his customer. The customer said, looking at his hair in the mirror,

> *Soko-wa moo sukoshi mijikaku.*
> (Make that place a little shorter, please.)

Then the barber said

> *A, koko-desu-ne. Konokurai-desu-ka.*
> (This part? About this much?)

and the customer answered

> *Un, sono kurai.*
> (Yes, about that much.)

Mr. Lerner was interested in the use of *koko* and *kono*, and of *soko* and *sono*. The customer used *soko* and *sono* although he was referring to his own hair, and the barber said *koko* and *kono* when referring to somebody else's hair.

*　　　　*　　　　*

The difference between *kono* and *sono* (or, between *koko* and *soko*) is that *kono* is used to refer to what is close to the speaker and *sono* is used to refer to what is close to the listener. Thus, one usually says

> *Kore, doozo.*

(Please take this.)

when handing something to someone. And you will ask someone

Sumimasen. Soko-no hon, totte-kudasaimasen-ka.

(I'm sorry to trouble you, but could you please hand me the book there?)

The distinction of whether something is close to the speaker or to the listener is not just a matter of physical distance but also of the relationship to the person. Therefore, when the barber was cutting the customer's hair, the hair was closely related to the barber, and even the owner of the hair, namely the customer, regarded it as belonging to the barber at the moment. Thus the customer used *sono* and the barber used *kono*.

In the same way, when you ask someone to give a message to another person, you should say *Koo tsutaete-kudasaimasen-ka* (Will you tell him this?) before stating the message, and *Soo tsutaete-kudasaimasen-ka* after stating it. The idea is that the message belongs to you before you pass it on, and afterward it belongs to the listener.

When reporting someone's statement, one usually says *Tanaka-san-ga soo iimashita* (Mr. Tanaka said so). However, you can also say *Tanaka-san-ga koo iimashita* (Mr. Tanaka said this) when you feel that you are still concerned with the statement and have not yet completely handed the matter over to the listener.

Gobusata-itashimashita
ごぶさたいたしました
(I'm sorry I have been neglecting to see you and write to you)

The other day Mr. Lerner visited Professor Takahashi, whom he had not seen for several weeks. Professor Takahashi said

Hisashiburi-desu-ne.
久しぶりですね。
(I haven't seen you for a long time.)

So Mr. Lerner answered

Kochira-koso.
(I should say that.)

The fact is that Mr. Lerner had learned that one should say *Gobusata-itashimashita* when meeting someone after a long time and that the answer to this expression is *Kochira-koso.* He thought that *Hisashiburi-desu-ne* must be a synonym for *Gobusata-itashimashita,* and so said *Kochira-koso* in reply. But when he asked Miss Yoshida about it later, she said he should have said

Hontoo-desu-ne.
ほんとうですね。
(That's certainly true.)

instead.

*　　　*　　　*

The two expressions *Hisashiburi-desu-ne* and *Gobusata-itashimashita* are similar but not the

102

same. *Hisashiburi-desu-ne* simply means that the two have not met for a long time, and is usually used as an expression of joy at meeting someone. Therefore one usually replies with such expressions as *Soo-desu-ne* and *Hontoo-ni soo-desu-ne*.

On the other hand *Gobusata-itashimashita* is an expression of apology for not having written or called on the other person. The complete version is

Gobusata-itashimashite, mooshiwake arima-sen.

(I'm so sorry that I have not written to you or seen you.)

but *mooshiwake arimasen* is often understood and left out. Between friends, a less polite expression, *Gobusata-shite, doomo* is used to mean the same thing.

The underlying idea in this sort of situation is that one should try to keep in contact with the other person and one should be sorry about neglecting to do so. In formal situations or in polite conversation in Japanese it is regarded as good to be ready to take blame on oneself and apologize. Therefore, to be polite *Gobusata-itashimashita* is more appropriate than *Hisashiburi-desu-ne*; *Hisashiburi-desu-ne* should be followed by *Gobusata-itashimashita* when one has to be polite.

Otoko-wa nyooboo-da
男は女房だ
(A man is a wife?)

Mr. Lerner and his colleagues were talking about Mr. Kobayashi, one of the youngest workers at the company, during lunchtime yesterday. Mr. Kobayashi recently got married and has become more enthusiastic about his work since then. Apparently his wife has had a good influence on him. Mr. Takada referred to this fact, and said, as if to give his conclusion

> *Otoko-wa nyooboo-dane.*
> 男は　女房だね。
> (*lit.* A man is a wife.)

and everybody agreed.

Mr. Lerner understood that Mr. Takada had meant that a wife is the most important factor in deciding a husband's way of living, but wondered if the use of . . . *wa* . . . *da* can be flexible to this extent.

*　　　*　　　*

A-*wa* B-*desu* (or -*da*) is often understood to mean "A is B," but actually this structure can be used in a much broader way.

A sentence which is often quoted to illustrate this aspect of the . . . *wa* . . . *desu* structure is

> *Boku-wa unagi-de.*
> (*lit.* I am an eel.)

which means "I will have eel" when said to a waiter taking one's order at a restaurant.

You can take this sentence to be the abbreviasion of

> *Boku-wa unagi-o taberu-n-desu.*
> (I'm going to eat some eel.)

or

> *Boku-ga taberu-nowa unagi-desu.*
> (It is eel that I am going to eat.)

Here the word *taberu* is understood and left out.

In the same way, *Otoko-wa nyooboo-da* can be paraphrased as

> *Otoko-wa nyooboo-ni yotte kimaru.*
> (What a man is like is determined by his wife.)

or

> *Otoko-o kimeru-nowa nyooboo-da.*
> (It is the wife who determines the man.)

There are several other examples of this kind which can easily be understood from context.

> *Yakyuu-wa pitchaa-desu.*
> (What counts most in baseball is the pitcher.)
> *Otoko-wa kao-ja nai. Kokoro-da.*
> 男は 顔じゃ ない。心だ。
> (A man's worth is not determined by his looks, but by his heart.)

Moo demashita
もう　出ました
(It has already left)

Mr. Lerner and Miss Yoshida arranged to meet at a bus stop after work yesterday evening. Miss Yoshida came five minutes late, and a bus left just before she came. Mr. Lerner told her

Basu-wa moo dekakemashita.

meaning "The bus has already left." But Miss Yoshida laughed and said that he should have said . . . *demashita* instead of . . . *dekakemashita*. He had not thought about the difference between *deru* and *dekakeru* before.

* * *

There are several verbs meaning that something or someone is leaving a place. *Shuppatsu-suru* is used when the time of departure is important, as in

Kono ressha-wa sanji-ni shuppatsu-shimasu.
(This train will leave at three.)

Deru can also be used in the above sentence, but it places the emphasis on leaving as in

Konde-kita-kara demashoo.
混んできたから　出ましょう。
(Since this place has become crowded, let's leave.)

Both *shuppatsu-suru* and *deru* can be used either with human beings or with inanimate things like trains, but the verb *dekakeru* is used only with human beings. *Dekakeru* is usually said when a person leaves his home to go to a place for some specific purpose, as in

> *Sanpo-ni dekakemashoo-ka.*
> 散歩に　出かけましょうか。
> (Shall we go out for a walk?)
> *Nichiyoobi-niwa amari dekakemasen.*
> (I don't go out very much on Sundays.)

Saying *Basu-wa moo dekakemashita* sounds as if the bus were a human being going out on special business. Other Japanese verbs are also used only with human beings, and using them for inanimate things or animals will sound funny. For instance, *kurasu* (to live) is used only with human beings. Actually it means "a human being lives his life." You cannot say something like

> *Kono doobutsuen-niwa nitoo-no zoo-ga kurashite-imasu.*
> (There are two elephants in this zoo.)

unless you want to personify the elephants.

Kiree-ni taberu
きれいに食べる
(To eat up)

Mr. Lerner and several other people from the office went out for lunch together yesterday. When they had finished eating, Mr. Takada looked at Mr. Kobayashi's plate and said

> *Kiree-ni tabeta-nee.*
> きれいに　食べたねえ。
> (*lit.* You ate beautifully.)

While Mr. Lerner was wondering what he meant, everybody agreed and admired Mr. Kobayashi's healthy digestion. All the others had left part of their food. Mr. Lerner wondered if *kiree-ni* means "completely."

*　　*　　*

The word *kiree* has several meanings. Most foreigners learn one of the meanings, "to be pretty or beautiful," first. When a person says

> *Kireena sora-desu-ne.*
> (The sky is beautiful.)
> *Kanojo kiree-ni natta-ne.*
> (She has become beautiful.)

he uses *kiree* in this sense.

Another meaning, "to be clean," is often used in everyday conversation as in

> *Te-o kiree-ni arainasai.*
> (Wash your hands well — so that they will become clean.)

And "to be tidy or neat" is also meant by *kiree,* as in

> *Tsukue-no ue-ga kiree-ni natta.*
> (The desk has been tidied up.)
> *Motto kiree-ni tatande-kudasai.*
> (Please fold it more neatly.)

When something is perfectly done, *kiree* is used as in

> *Shigoto-ga kiree-ni katazuita.*
> 仕事が　きれいに　かたづいた。
> (The work is completely finished.)

And as in Mr. Kobayashi's case, eating something all up is described as

> *Kiree-ni taberu.*
> (To eat up.)

All in all, *kiree* describes the speaker's satisfaction at seeing something in an ideal, good state; thus the word can correspond to such English adjectives as "pretty," "clean," "tidy," "neat" and "complete."

Some foreigners make the mistake of saying *kireekatta* for *kiree-deshita* to mean "it was pretty"; *kiree* is used with *na* before a noun, as in *kireena sora.* And to make it negative you should say *kiree-ja arimasen* or *kiree-ja nai* instead of *kireeku nai,* which Japanese children sometimes used before they learn the correct form.

Itte-mo ii-kedo . . .
行っても いいけど……
(I don't mind going, but . . .)

When Mr. Lerner and Miss Yoshida were talking at lunchtime yesterday, someone called Miss
Yoshida. It was obviously a friend of hers asking
her to go to a movie. Miss Yoshida said

> *Itte-mo ii-kedo, ima nani yatteru-no.*
> 行っても いいけど、今 何 やってるの。
> (I don't mind going, but what's on now?)

Mr. Lerner had not realized that . . . *te-mo ii* can
be used to refer to the action of the speaker and
wondered how much interest the speaker shows
in that action when he uses it.

*　　*　　*

The expression . . . *te-mo ii* is usually used
for giving permission, as in

> *Moo kaette-mo ii-desu-yo.*
> (You may go home now.)

or for asking for permission as in

> *Moo kaette-mo ii-desu-ka.*
> (May I go home now?)

There are, however, several other usages of
this expression. To mention one, it can also be
used with the first person as in Miss Yoshida's
case. This roughly corresponds to the English "I
don't mind . . . ing" or "I might as well . . ." as
in

110

A: *Kore, saki-ni yatte-kuremasen-ka.*
(Would you do this first?)
B: *Ee, saki-ni shite-mo ii-desu-yo.*
(OK. I don't mind doing it first.)

A: *Issho-ni itte-kuremasen-ka.*
(Will you go with me?)
B: *Itte-mo ii-kedo, saki-ni kaeru-kamo shirenai-yo.*
I don't mind going, but I may have to leave early.)

As seen in the examples, this expression implies that the speaker is not very positive. Therefore it cannot be used when accepting an offer or agreeing to do a favor in polite situations. To be polite, one has to choose other expressions that show more enthusiasm.

111

Bakari
ばかり
(About; Only)

When Mr. Takada asked Miss Yoshida how her brother was doing, she answered

Asonde-bakari-ite komaru-n-desu.
遊んでばかりいて　困るんです。
(He is just enjoying himself and does not study — so I am worried.)

just like most sisters of high school students preparing for exams to get into college. Mr. Lerner realized that *bakari* means "only" here.

Then Mr. Takada told her

Jippun-bakari rusu-ni suru-kara . . .
(I'm going out for about 10 minutes.)

He wondered how Japanese can tell whether *bakari* means "only" or "about."

*　　　*　　　*

The word *bakari* is used in two meanings, "only" and "about." When *bakari* is added to a word indicating an amount, it means "about" as in

Sen-en-bakari kashite-kuremasen-ka.
(Will you lend me about 1,000 yen?)
Nikagetsu-bakari kakarimasu.
(It will take about two months.)

When *bakari* is used with words other than those indicating an amount, it means "nothing but" or "only." As in Miss Yoshida's remark about her brother, it is used with verbs as in

Mainichi sake-o nonde-bakari-iru.
(He does nothing but drink every day.)

It is also added to a noun as in

Mainichi sake-bakari nonde-iru.

which means either "Every day he drinks nothing but alcoholic beverages" or "He does nothing but drink every day" depending on the context.

When *bakari* is used with the past form of a verb, it means that an action has just been completed and it is still too early to expect a certain result. For instance, saying

Sengetsu koko-e kita-bakari-desu.
(I came here only last month.)

implies such things as that the speaker does not know the geography of the neighborhood or is not settled yet. Also, if one says

Ima ohiru-o tabeta-bakari-desu.
(I have just had lunch.)

it implies either that he is not yet ready to resume his work or that he is so full that he does not care to eat anything else.

Tomarimasu-ka
とまりますか
(Are you going to stay overnight?)

Mr. Lerner and Miss Yoshida were invited to the Takadas' last Saturday. Mrs. Takada told them that she had to go to Kyushu the following day to attend the wedding of a relative. Mr. Lerner wondered if she was coming back on the same day, and asked,

Kyuushuu-e itte, soko-de nemasu-ka.

meaning "Are you going to sleep over in Kyushu?" But Mrs. Takada blushed, Mr. Takada laughed, and Miss Yoshida hurriedly said as if to cover up Mr. Lerner's blunder

Achira-de otomari-ni naru-n-desu-ka.
あちらで おとまりに なるんですか。
(Are you going to stay overnight there?)

*　　　*　　　*

Mr. Lerner's question was inappropriate because it sounded as if Mrs. Takada were going to Kyushu to have some love affair. He should have used the word *tomaru* instead of *neru* in this case. To say overnight at somewhere, one says *tomaru* as in

Kyooto-de hitoban tomarimashita.
(I stayed overnight in Kyoto.)
Yamada-san-no otaku-ni futaban tomarimashita.
(I stayed with the Yamadas for two nights.)

The English "sleep over" should not be translated as *neru* in Japanese. In a similar way, there are several other expressions one should be careful about.

The expression *osewa-ni naru* means "to be treated kindly" as in

> *Iroiro osewa-ni narimashita.*
> (Thank you very much for your kind help.)

or

> *Kyuushuu-e itta toki Yamada-san-ni osewa-ni narimashita.*
> (Mr. Yamada kindly helped me when I went down to Kyushu.)

But saying *Yamada-san-no osewa-ni natte-imasu* can be misleading; especially when the speaker is a woman and Mr. Yamada is a wealthy middle-aged man, the implication can be that the speaker is Mr. Yamada's mistress.

Kankee-ga aru (to have relations) can also be misleading when it is used to refer to the relationship between two people of the opposite sex. And such simple words as *otoko* (man) and *onna* (woman) can mean one's lover depending on the context. To avoid this danger, you should say *otoko-no-hito* and *onna-no-hito* instead.

Onna-no-hito-ga kimashita means "There's a woman to see you," but saying

> *Onna-ga kimashita* implies that she is someone's mistress.

Issho-ni shimashoo
いっしょに　しましょう
(Let's do it together)

Mr. Lerner received a letter from his sister Margaret asking him to visit a couple named Maeda whom she had met in the United States. They were studying at an American university and had recently returned to Japan. Both of them are now working for big companies, so Mr. Lerner went to visit them in the evening. When he reached their apartment, Mr. Maeda was not yet home, and Mrs. Maeda was busily preparing dinner. She asked him to wait in the living room and served him a cup of tea. But Mr. Lerner wanted to help her, and he also wanted to have a conversation with her, so he said

Issho-ni shitaku-o shimashoo.
(Let's fix dinner together.)

Mrs. Maeda looked surprised and said no, and added that there was not much to do. Mr. Lerner repeated Issho-ni shimashoo, soshite issho-ni hanashimashoo (Let's do it together and talk together). But she looked embarrassed and even a little offended. Mr. Lerner wondered if letting a man help with housework is still regarded as inappropriate in Japan.

*   *   *

Mrs. Maeda objected not to having a man help but to having a guest do so. Okyakusama, a visitor, has to be treated with special care, and if the visitor has never been there before, as in Mr. Lerner's case, a Japanese hostess does not let him help her. This is true even if the visitor is a woman, although the hostess' reaction to the proposal of help might be different with a woman visitor.

And if Mr. Lerner's expression had been different, Mrs. Maeda would not have felt so offended. A Japanese guest would use a much more reserved expression such as

Nanika otetsudai dekiru koto-wa nai-deshooka.

何か お手伝い できる ことは ないでしょうか。

(I wonder if there is anything I can do to help you.)

rather than *Issho-ni shimashoo.*

Both *issho-ni* and . . . *mashoo* are usually taught to foreigners as basic expressions, but *issho-ni* . . . *mashoo* sounds so familiar that it cannot be used in polite situations. Mr. Lerner would have used a more reserved expression in his native tongue, but when speaking a foreign language anyone is apt to use what he has learned first. Such expressions might be called "classroom Japanese" and they have to be used with care in social situations.

Uchi-no akachan
うちの　あかちゃん
(Our baby)

Mr. Takada was talking with Miss Yoshida about his baby at lunchtime yesterday. When he said

> *Uchi-no akanboo-ga netsu-o dashite* . . .
> うちの　あかんぼうが　熱を　出して……
> (Our baby has a fever.)

Miss Yoshida looked worried and said

> *Akachan-ga . . . Maa kawaisoo-ni.*
> あかちゃんが……まあ　かわいそうに。
> (Your baby? Oh, the poor thing.)

While listening to them, Mr. Lerner realized that Mr. Takada always said *akanboo* while Miss Yoshida said *akachan*; he wondered if it was because the baby belonged to the Takadas or because men and women use different words.

＊　　　＊　　　＊

The word *akachan* is used as a polite term to refer to someone else's baby while *akanboo* is used as a humble term to refer to one's own baby or as a general term meaning "baby."

To refer to someone else's baby, one uses *akachan* as in

> *Otaku-no akachan, ogenki-desu-ka.*
> (How's your baby?)
> *Yamada-san-no tokoro-ni akachan-ga umareta-soo-desu.*
>
> (I hear a baby was born to the Yamadas.)

On the other hand, when referring to one's own baby in social situations, one usually says *akanboo* as in

Sengetsu akanboo-ga umaremashita.
(A baby was born to us last month.)
Uchi-no akanboo-wa mada sankagetsu-desu.
(Our baby is only three months old.)

It is all right for a child to say *uchi-no akachan,* but it is usually regarded as childish for an adult to say this when talking with non-family members. The ending *-chan* is not added to the names of one's own family members when referring to them in social situations; therefore saying *uchi-no akachan* is just as immature as saying *Yoshiko-chan* when referring to one's daughter in public.

When one refers to babies in general, *akanboo* is used as in

Kono-goro akanboo-no kaze-ga hayatte-iru soo-da.
(I hear colds are spreading among babies now.)

But when one has a personal interest in babies, one tends to use *akachan* even when referring to babies in general; some women, for example, use *akachan* in this way.

Kanai
家内
(My wife)

Mr. Lerner wanted to invite Mr. and Mrs. Takada to his house some time and asked Mr. Takada when would be a good time for them. Mr. Takada answered,

Ja, konban soodan-shite-mimasu.
じゃ、今晩 相談してみます。
(Well, I will talk about it with her this evening.)

Mr. Lerner wondered if it is also correct to say
. . . *kanai-ni soodan-shite-mimasu.*

*　　　*　　　*

There are several terms used to refer to one's wife in social situations, and one has to choose the appropriate one depending on the situation. But often one does not use any term at all to refer to his wife. In the case mentioned above, Mr. Takada did not have to say . . . *kanai-ni* because it was obvious from the context that he was referring to his wife. In this kind of situation one can also say

Uchi-de soodan-shite-mimasu.
(*lit.* I will talk about it at home.)

because it is obvious that one is going to talk about it with one's wife.

Among the several words one uses when it is necessary to refer to one's wife in a social situation, *kanai* is the most common, as in

Kanai-ga yoroshiku-to mooshite-orimashita.

家内が　よろしくと　申しておりました。

(My wife asked me to give you her best wishes.)

Needless to say, *okusan* or *uchi-no okusan* cannot be used in public because *okusan* is an honorific term.

Several foreigners say that some Japanese laugh when they use *kanai* and they wonder why. It is difficult to judge without knowing each situation precisely, but there are two possible reasons. One is that they may have used *kanai* in very informal situations; *kanai* sounds rather formal, and in informal situations Japanese men use various other terms such as *nyooboo*, *uchi-no*, *uchi-no yatsu*, etc., depending on the situation and their personal taste.

Another possible reason is that they may have used *kanai* more often than necessary. It sounds strange to say *kanai* when a Japanese would not use any term at all to refer to his wife, and if the speaker happens to be a newlywed, he might become the object of a teasing smile.

Ii toshi
いい年
(Good age)

When Mr. Lerner was talking with his colleagues at lunchtime yesterday, Mr. Takada started talking about retirement, explaining what plans he had for after he was retired. Miss Yoshida said that his plans seemed fine, but that it was too early for him to think about retirement. Then he answered

Iya, boku-mo ii toshi-da-kara-ne.
いや、ぼくも いい 年だからね。
(*lit.* No, because I am already at a good age.)

Mr. Lerner wondered what he meant by *ii toshi*.

* * *

The expression *ii toshi* is used to mean that one is old enough to start doing something. The implication differs depending on the context. For instance, when an adult is seen engaged in a childish pastime, someone may say

Ii toshi-o shite sonna asobi-o . . .
(You're too old for such a pastime.)

Or, one may complain about someone for his lack of consideration as in

Ii toshi-o shite bakana koto-o shita mon-da.
(He should know better at his age.)

Mr. Takada meant that he was old enough to

start thinking about retirement when he said *boku-mo ii toshi-da*. In a similar way one sometimes comments, about a young person being already at a marriageable age,

> *Ano-ko-mo moo ii toshi-da-ne.*
> (He/She is old enough to get married now.)

The word *ii* is also used with other nouns to mean "good enough." When one looks at his watch and says

> *Oya, moo ii jikan-da.*
> おや、もう　いい　時間だ。

he means that it is high time he start doing something like taking his leave or going back to work. Similarly a mother will say to her child

> *Moo ii jikan-desu-yo.*

meaning "you should get up," "you should go to bed," "you should start studying," or so on.

Ii-desu-ne. Demo warui-desu-ne.
いいですね。でも わるいですね。
(It's good, but it's bad)

Last Friday evening Mr. Lerner and several people from the office went to a bar and had some beer together. When they left the bar, Mr. Lerner asked them to come to his house, which happened to be rather close, and eat something. Someone said

> Ii-desu-ne. Demo warui-desu-ne.
> いいですね。でも わるいですね。
> (*lit.* It's good, but it's bad.)

Then Mr. Takada said

> Warui-kedo, sore-ga ii-yo.
> わるいけど、それが いいよ。
> (*lit.* It's bad, but it's good.)

and they decided to accept Mr. Lerner's offer.

＊　　　＊　　　＊

In this case Ii-desu-ne and Warui-desu-ne do not have their literal meaning of "It is good" and "It is bad." The expression Ii-desu-ne is used to mean "That's a very good idea, so I will do so" when accepting someone's offer. (Saying Ii-desu can mean "No, thank you," but Ii-desu-ne indicates acceptance.) Warui-desu-ne is the abbreviation of "It's not good for me to trouble you" or "I shouldn't trouble you." When these two expressions are combined as Ii-desu-ne, demo warui-desu-ne, it actually means "That's good, so I will accept, although I feel bad at troubling you." Reversing the order of the two expressions as *Warui-kedo, sore-ga ii* also means the same thing, although this sounds more positive about accepting the offer.

Warui-desu-ne is often used when one is going to accept someone's kindness, as in

A: *Watashi-no kasa, motte-ttara doo-desu-ka.*
   (Why don't you take my umbrella?)
B: *Soo-desu-ka. Warui-desu-ne. Doomo.*
   (May I? That's kind of you. Thanks.)

In more familiar conversation between friends, men will say *Warui-ne* and women *Warui-wane*. To be polite, one uses more reserved expressions such as *Sumimasen(-ne)* or *Mooshiwake arimasen (-ne)* as in

Kekkoo-de-gozaimasu-ne, demo mooshiwake gozaimasen.
Kekkoo-desu-kedo, mooshiwake nai yoona ki-ga itashimasu.

both meaning "I will accept your offer, although I feel I shouldn't trouble you."

Hee?
へえ？
(Really?)

When Mr. Lerner was talking with his colleagues after lunch yesterday, Mr. Takada said that he was trying to quit smoking. Since he had already tried and failed in this several times, Mr. Lerner teased him by answering

Hee?
へえ？
(Really?)

But when he said it, everybody laughed. Mr. Lerner wondered if his pronunciation was wrong.

*　　　*　　　*

There are several expressions that are used as replies, either at the end of a sentence or between phrases. *Hai* is very common; it is polite, and can be used in formal situations too. When trying to be very polite, sometimes *Haa* is used in place of *Hai*. Sometimes a short *Ha* is used, mostly by men and especially when replying to their boss. *Aa* is also used. This sounds similar to *Haa* but is casual and familiar; you should not use it toward someone you have to talk politely with.

Ee is less polite than *Hai*, and often used in informal conversation. *Hee*, however, is quite different from *Ee*, although there is the difference of only one consonant. When said with a falling tone as in

He
　e

it is used as a humble, even subservient, answer toward one's superior. It often reminds one of a peasant timidly answering a samurai or a servant in an old-fashioned rich family replying to his master. Nowadays it is rarely used in Tokyo.

On the other hand, when said with a rising tone as in

e

He

it indicates the speaker's doubt, surprise or contempt about what has been said. Mr. Lerner wanted to use *Hee* in this way, but he used a falling tone by mistake.

Fuun can also be used as a response to indicate that one is interested in what the other person has said, while the short *Fun* often indicates contempt or quick dismissal.

Hoo is also used to indicate one's interest or surprise, usually by elderly men.

The response words mentioned above — *Hai, Haa, Ee, Fuun, Fun* and *Hoo* — are sometimes repeated, as in *Hai, hai* or in *Hoo, hoo* when said with a falling tone, to emphatically express one's interest.

Wakaru dokoro-ka . . .
わかる どころか……
(Far from being able to understand . . .)

The other day Miss Yoshida introduced Mr. Lerner to her uncle, who had come to see her at the office. The uncle politely bowed to him, and then asked Miss Yoshida if he understood Japanese. She answered

> *Wakaru dokoro-ka . . .*
> わかる どころか……
> (Far from being able to understand it . . .)

Then the uncle looked at Mr. Lerner with an admiring look and wondered how he had become so good at it.

This was quite puzzling to Mr. Lerner. Hadn't she denied his ability to understand Japanese?

*   *   *

The expressions . . . *dokoro-ka* is used to deny the appropriateness of what has been said. It can mean that what has been said is quite wrong, as in

A: *Densha, konde-imashita-ka.*
 (Was the train crowded?)
B: *Konde-iru dokoro-ka garagara-deshita.*
 (Far from being crowded, there were very few passengers on it.)
or,
 Oishii-to iwarete katta-n-desu-ga, oishii dokoro-ka hidoi mon-deshita.
 (They told me it was good, so I bought it, but far from being delicious, it was really terrible.)

128

This expression is also used to correct the wording that has been used to describe something. When Miss Yoshida said *Wakaru dokoro-ka*, she meant that the expression *wakaru* is not appropriate to describe Mr. Lerner's ability. If she had completed her sentence, it would have been something like

Wakaru dokoro-ka marude nihonjin-mitai-desu.
(Far from being able to just understand it, he can speak it as well as a native speaker of Japanese.)
Wakaru dokoro-ka joodan-made ieru-n-desu-yo.
(Far from being able to just understand it, he can even make jokes in Japanese.)

Her uncle understood that she was praising Mr. Lerner's ability before she completed her sentence, because it would be inconceivable to use this expression in the opposite way, namely to mean that Mr. Lerner is an extremely poor speaker of Japanese, in a social situation.

In the same way, you might answer someone who has asked you if the train was crowded

Konde-iru dokoro-ka shinu omoi-deshita.
(Crowded isn't the word. I almost died!)

Yamada-san-de irasshaimasu-ka
山田さんで いらっしゃいますか
(Are you Mr. Yamada?)

Yesterday afternoon Mr. Lerner and Mr. Takada went to see a Mr. Yamada at his office. When they were led to his desk, and he stood up to meet them, Mr. Takada bowed and said

Yamada-san-de irasshaimasu-ka.
山田さんで いらっしゃいますか。

Mr. Lerner thought that he had said

Yamada-san irasshaimasu-ka.
(Is Mr. Yamada here?)

and was wondering why, when the man replied *Soo-desu* (That's right) and asked them to sit down.

*   *   *

The two expressions . . . *de irasshaimasu-ka* and . . . *irasshaimasu-ka* are quite different. The former means "Are you . . .?" and the latter means "Is . . . here?" While *irassharu* means "to exist," . . . *de irassharu* means "to be equal to . . ." Actually . . . *de irasshaimasu* is a polite version of . . . *desu* while *irasshaimasu* is the polite form of *imasu*.

Ogenki-desu-ka.
お元気ですか。

and

Ogenki-de irasshaimasu-ka.
お元気で いらっしゃいますか。

both mean "Are you well?" The latter is more polite than the former. Mr. Takada said *Yamada-san-de irasshaimasu-ka* instead of . . . *desu-ka* because he wanted to speak politely.

There are several ways to refer to someone's action politely. For instance, one can say

Nanji-goro kaerimasu-ka.

to mean "What time are you (is he, is she, are they) coming back?" To make this more polite one says

Nanji-goro okaeri-ni narimasu-ka.

Instead of *o . . . ni narimasu-ka,* one often uses *o . . . desu-ka* as in

Nanji-goro okaeri-desu-ka.

This is shorter but still sounds polite and refined. To make this even more polite, one says

Nanji-goro okaeri-de irasshaimasu-ka.

In the same way, such expressions are often used in polite conversations as:

Oisogi-de irasshaimasu-ka.
(Are you in a hurry?)
Osuki-de irasshaimasu-ka.
(Do you like it?)

In the case of such adjectives as *hayai, wakai,* etc., . . . *kute irasshaimasu* is used as in

Owakakute irasshaimasu-ne.
(You are so young.)

Takaku nai-ja nai
たかく　ないじゃ　ない
(It isn't expensive, is it?)

Miss Yoshida showed her new handbag to another woman working at the office, complaining that it was rather expensive. The woman praised its quality and said

> *Takaku nai-ja nai.*
> たかく　ないじゃ　ない。
> (*lit.* It isn't that it isn't expensive.)

Then Mr. Takada joined them and said

> *Takaku nai-ja nai-ka.*

From the situation Mr. Lerner imagined that they were saying that the handbag was not too expensive, but the use of . . . *ja nai* still seemed difficult to him.

*　　　*　　　*

Miss Yoshida's colleagues said that the handbag was not expensive. The last part of the sentence, namely *-ja nai,* does not change the meaning. It is something like a tag question with falling intonation in English. Thus the sentence

> *Takaku nai-ja nai(-ka).*

means "It isn't expensive, is it?"

If one wants to say that something is expensive one says

> *Takai-ja nai(-ka).*
> (It's expensive, isn't it?)

132

Men use either *nai* or *nai-ka*; the latter sounds more demanding. Women usually do not add *ka* to *nai*. To make the expression more polite, both men and women use . . . *ja arimasen-ka*; in this case, too, women sometimes leave out *ka*.

Using *nai* twice as in *Takaku nai-ja nai* may seem confusing to foreigners, but it actually is not. The first *nai,* which determines the meaning, is said clearly so that it gives the impression of finality, and the last *-ja nai* is felt to be an indication of the speaker's emotions. In the following sentences, the first *nai* or *nakatta* is said with a higher pitch and thus there is no ambiguity.

Ano-hito genki-ga nai-ja nai.
(He doesn't look very well, does he?)
Shibaraku awanakatta-ja nai.
(We haven't met for a long time, have we?)

Sometimes *nai* is said more than twice in the following example,

Dekinai koto-wa nai-ja nai.
できない　ことは　ないじゃ　ない。

(It isn't impossible, is it?)

Zenbu-wa wakarimasen-deshita
ぜんぶは　わかりませんでした
(I didn't understand all of it)

Mr. Lerner went to a Japanese movie with Miss Yoshida last Saturday. When they were having tea after the movie, Miss Yoshida asked him how well he had understood the movie. He answered

Zenbu wakarimasen-deshita.

but seeing the disappointed look on her face he realized his mistake and corrected himself by saying

Zenbu-wa wakarimasen-deshita.
ぜんぶは　わかりませんでした。

*   *   *

The Japanese words meaning "all" or "every" are usually followed by affirmative verbs as in

Zenbu owarimashita.
(I finished all of it.)
Minna kowarete-imasu.
(All of them are broken.)

It sounds strange to use these words with negative verbs as in

Zenbu owarimasen-deshita.
Minna kowarete-imasen.

To mean "not all" or "not every," one adds *wa* as in

134

Zenbu-wa owarimasen-deshita.
(I didn't finish all of it.)
Minna-wa kowarete-imasen.
(Not all of them are broken.)

The particle *wa* is added to various words which the speaker wants to call the listener's attention to or to show a special concern with. Thus one says

Kinoo-wa uchi-ni imashita.
(I stayed home yesterday.)

when one wants to emphasize *kinoo*. One may also say

Kinoo-wa watashi-wa uchi-ni imashita.

when one wants to call the listener's attention to both *kinoo* and *watashi*. Sometimes *wa* is used more than twice as in

Kinoo-wa watashi-wa uchi-niwa imashita-ga te-rebi-wa mimasen-deshita.
(I stayed home yesterday but I didn't watch TV.)

You might think of *wa* as being something like a spotlight; you can use it to highlight any part of a person or a thing on the stage. It is usually used to highlight just one spot, but it is possible to highlight more than one — for instance, a person's face and two hands.

Yokka-kara-desu-ka
四日からですか
(From the fourth?)

While Mr. Lerner and Mr. Takada were discussing some business with Mr. Mori, the director of the company, the latter said that he was going to Europe the following Friday and would be away from the office for a week. Mr. Lerner wanted to confirm the date and asked him

> *Yokka-kara?*
> (From the fourth?)

Before Mr. Mori answered, Mr. Takada asked the same question with a slightly different wording,

> *Yokka-kara-desu-ka.* 四日からですか。

Mr. Lerner wondered if he should have added *desu-ka* even after such a short phrase.

*　　　*　　　*

In polite conversation sentences usually end with *-masu* or *desu*, as in *Ashita ikimasu* (I'm going there tomorrow) or *Kinoo itta-n-desu* (I went there yesterday). Only in familiar conversation does one leave out *-masu* or *desu* as in

A: *Itsu iku-no.*
(When are you going there?)
B: *Ashita.*
(Tomorrow.)
or
A: *Itsu itta-no.*
(When did you go there?)

136

B: *Kinoo.*
   (Yesterday.)

In English conversation it is not especially impolite to give short answers such as "Tomorrow" or "Yesterday." But in Japanese conversation, when one has been speaking with *-masu* or *desu*, it sounds strange to suddenly shift to the familiar style by leaving out *-masu* or *desu*.

Desu is added not only to nouns and pronouns but also to phrases with particles such as

Ashita-kara-desu-ka.
(From tomorrow?)
Ashita-made-desu.
(Until tomorrow.)
Sannin-dake-desu.
(Just three people.)

Sometimes it is even added to phrases ending with *ni* or *de.*

I. A: *Dare-ni tanonda-n-desu-ka.*
       (Who did you ask to do it?)
    B: *Tanaka-san-ni-desu.*
       (Mr. Tanaka.)
II. A: *Eki-no mae-de matte-ite-kudasai.*
       (Please wait in front of the station.)
    B: *Eki-no mae-de-desu-ka.*
       (In front of the station?)
    A: *Ee, soo-desu.*
       (Yes, that's right.)

When a Japanese speaker suddenly stops using *desu* in the midst of a polite conversation, he has a special reason for doing so. The reason may be a strong emotion such as surprise, joy or anger on the part of the speaker or various other things. Unless you have a special reason, it is better to add *desu* to your phrases when talking politely.

137

Doomo umaku dekinai
どうも うまく できない
(Somehow I can't do it well)

When Mr. Lerner was having lunch with Mr. Takada the other day, they talked about several of their colleagues. Mr. Lerner was surprised to learn that Mr. Takada had a high opinion of Mr. Kato, who did not seem very capable to him. He had often noticed Mr. Kato complain about his work saying,

> *Doomo umaku ikanai.*
> どうも うまく いかない。
> (Somehow it doesn't go well.)

or

> *Doomo umaku dekinai.*
> どうも うまく できない。
> (Somehow I can't do it well.)

When Mr. Lerner referred to this fact, Mr. Takada asked him if he had actually witnessed any serious mistake by Mr. Kato. Mr. Lerner could not think of any. Then why is Mr. Kato complaining all the time? Is he self-conscious or hypocritical?

*　　　*　　　*

As is often mentioned, the Japanese usually deny any praise from others and devalue their own ability in social situations. To accept someone's praise too readily in a social situation is regarded as childish.

And sometimes people purposely complain about their own ability. This is often seen among senior members of a group, who are trusted and looked up to by younger members. These people often complain by saying things like

Kono-goro doomo wasureppoku natte komaru.
(These days I forget things so often.)
Doomo boku-wa atama-ga warui mon-da-kara, nakanaka wakaranakute . . .
(I am so slow to understand things.)

The underlying idea is that an influential person should act so as to conceal his power and put the weaker members at ease. It is usually regarded as good and even considerate for an in fluential person to occasionally show his weaknesses. Needless to say the weakness should not be a vital one, but it is better to have some weaknesses than to be perfectly strong and consequently overly powerful or intimidating.

This idea is related to the popular liking of clumsy speech on the part of eminent statesmen in Japan. It is said that the late Masayoshi Ohira was a very fluent speaker when he was an offi cial working for the Ministry of Finance, but when he became prime minister, he started, on someone's advice, to talk in a faltering way with frequent "er's."

Tanaka-san-kara denwa-ga arimashita
田中さんから 電話が ありました
(There was a telephone call from Mr. Tanaka)

Yesterday afternoon Mr. Lerner answered a phone call from a Mr. Tanaka for Miss Yoshida, who was not in the office at the moment. When she came back, Mr. Lerner said

Tanaka-san-ga denwa-shimashita.

meaning "Mr. Tanaka called you." She thanked him and then corrected his wording saying

"Tanaka-san-kara denwa-ga atta" . . . *de-shoo?*
(You mean 'There was a telephone call from Mr. Tanaka'?)

* * *

Saying *Tanaka-san-ga denwa-shimashita* sounds strange in an actual conversation because it sounds as if Mr. Tanaka called someone other than the speaker and the listener. If you mean to say that Mr. Tanaka called the listener, you should say

Tanaka-san-kara denwa-ga arimashita.
田中さんから 電話が ありました。
(There was a telephone call from Mr. Tanaka.)

Or, if you use the word *denwa-suru* or *denwa-o kakeru,* you should say

Tanaka-san-ga denwa-shite-kimashita.
    or
Tanaka-san-ga denwa-o kakete-kimashita.

In these two sentences, . . . *te-kimashita* indicates that the telephone call was directed to the speaker or the listener. When *kakete-kimashita* or *shite-kimashita* is pronounced in one breath, it just means that Mr. Tanaka called and it does not mean that he actually came. If one pronounces the phrase with a pause in the middle, as in

Tanaka-san-ga denwa-o kakete (or shite) . . . kimashita.

it means that he called and then came.
    Sometimes *kakaru* is also used as in

Tanaka-san-kara denwa-ga kakatte-kimashita.

And if you have answered the phone and it is for someone else, you should say to that person

Denwa-desu.
(It's for you; *lit.* It's the telephone.)
    or, more politely,
Odenwa-desu.

You can mention the caller's name as in

Tanaka-san-kara denwa-desu.
(It's a call from Mr. Tanaka.)

If the recipient of the call is nearby and has seen you pick up the receiver, you can just say

Tanaka-san-desu.
(It's Mr. Tanaka.)

Ki-ni shinai, ki-ni shinai
気に　しない、気に　しない。
(Don't worry!)

Yesterday evening Mr. Lerner and several colleagues went to have some beer after work. Mr. Takada offered to pay because he had recently earned some extra money. When the others hesitated to accept his offer, he said

> Ki-ni shinai, ki-ni shinai.
> 気に　しない、気に　しない。
> (*lit.* Not to worry, not to worry.)

Mr. Lerner did not understand at first; he had learned that when the subject is not mentioned the sentence usually refers to the speaker, but this must be different.

*　　*　　*

The plain negative form is sometimes used as an imperative in familiar conversation. *Ki-ni shinai* corresponds to "You don't worry!" or "Don't worry!" in English. This form is often repeated, as in *Ki-ni shinai, ki-ni shinai*. For example, when good friends start to disagree, one will sometimes say jokingly

> Okoranai, okoranai.
> おこらない、おこらない。

meaning "Don't become angry!" Or a mother will sometimes say to her child

> Moo nakanai, nakanai.
> (Don't cry any more.)

The affirmative form can also be used as a familiar command, but then it is usually in the past form as in

Atchi-e itta, itta.
(Go away, will you?)
Saa, nonda, nonda.
(Go ahead and drink!)

Using these forms as a command is more common among men than among women. Except when a mother is talking to her child, women usually prefer . . . *te* or . . . *naide* to make a request as in *Atchi-e itte* or *Ikanaide*, although these forms are also used by men.

To make this expression softer in tone, *ne* is often added as in *Itte-ne* or *Ikanaide-ne*; if *yo* is used, it usually implies emphasis or irritation as in

Hayaku itte-yo.
(Go right now, please!)
Sore-wa iwanaide-yo, onegai-da-kara.
(Won't you please stop mentioning that?)

143

"Tooka?" "Deshita."
「十日？」「でした」
(The tenth? Yes.)

Mr. Takada was talking with someone on the phone, reporting that the director of the company had returned from Europe. While talking, he turned to Miss Yoshida, who was nearby, to make sure of the date, saying

Tooka? 十日？
(The tenth?)

and she answered briefly

Deshita. でした。
(It was.)

Mr. Lerner was interested in this short answer, and wondered if this was possible with other words too.

* * *

This way of answering a question can be used with any form ending a sentence. Besides *deshita,* such endings as *desu-ne* and *deshoo-ne* are often used as in

"*Tooka?*" "*Deshoo-ne.*" (The tenth? Probably.)
"*Tooka?*" "*Desu-ne.*" (The tenth? Yes, it is.)

The ending can be very short as well as fairly long.

"*Tooka?*" "*Deshita.*"
(The tenth? Yes, it was.)

144

"Tooka-datta?" "To omoimasu."
(It was the tenth? Yes, I think so.)
"Tooka-datta?" "Kamo shiremasen."
(It was the tenth? Maybe.)
"Tooka?" "Datta-kamo shiremasen."
(The tenth? Yes, it may have been.)
"Tooka?" "Datta yoona ki-ga shimasu-kedo-ne."
(The tenth? Yes, it seems to me it was the tenth.)

As is seen in the above examples, the question and the answer make up one complete sentence; in other words, the second speaker finishes the incomplete sentence started by the first speaker. And in group conversation one sentence can be split into more than two parts, as in

A: *Are-wa tashika tooka?*
B: *Datta yoona ki-ga shimasu.*
C: *Kedo-ne.*
(If my memory is correct, that was the tenth, wasn't it?)

This type of talking is common in conversation between those who share the same feelings about the topic, and it helps build up good relations between them. A typical conversation of this kind will be something like:

A: *Kore-wa moshika suru-to kojin-no mondai-ja nakute*
B: *Mushiro shakai-no*
C: *Shakai zentai-no mondai-to shite*
D: *Toraeru beki-deshoo-ne.*
A: *Ee, soo-deshoo-ne.*
(This problem should not be regarded as one concerning individuals but as one concerning the society as a whole.)

Kaetta hoo-ga ii
帰った ほうが いい
(You had better go home)

Mr. Lerner noticed that Miss Yoshida did not look well when she was typing yesterday afternoon. When he asked her if she was all right, she said that she had caught a cold, so he said

Moo kaeru hoo-ga ii-desu-yo.

meaning ''You had better go home now.'' Then Mr. Takada came and joined him, saying

Moo kaetta hoo-ga ii-yo.
もう 帰った ほうが いいよ。

Mr. Lerner wondered if he should have said *kaetta* instead of *kaeru*.

*　　*　　*

Both *Kaeru hoo-ga ii* and *Kaetta hoo-ga ii* are grammatically correct, but the speaker's attitude is different. When one says *Kaeru hoo-ga ii,* he states his judgment; he thinks that going home is better than not going home. On the other hand, when one says *Kaetta hoo-ga ii,* he is advising the listener to go home.

In this way, verbs in the past form are used to give advice, as in

Sugu dekaketa hoo-ga ii-deshoo.
(You had better leave right away.)
Kusuri-o nonda hoo-ga ii-desu-yo.
(You had better take some medicine.)

It is not easy to give advice politely. When

146

one uses this . . . *ta (da) hoo-ga ii* expression in polite situations, one has to change the verb into the *o . . . -ni naru* form as in

Sugu odekake-ni natta hoo-ga ii-deshoo.
すぐ お出かけに なった ほうが いいでしょう。
(It might be better if you left right away.)

And sometimes the last part of the sentence is also changed as in

Kusuri-o onomi-ni natta hoo-ga yoroshii-ka-to omoimasu.
(It might be better if you took some medicine.)

Or, one often avoids using . . . *ta(da) hoo-ga ii* and uses some other expression instead such as

Sugu odekake-ni nattara ikaga-deshoo.
(Wouldn't it be better if you left right away?)
Kusuri-o onomi-ni natte-wa ikaga-deshoo.
(Wouldn't it be better if you took some medicine?)

GENERAL INDEX

Volumes 1—5

I. **SITUATIONAL EXPRESSIONS** 150
Advice
Apology
Asking about wishes
Daily greetings
Disapproval, Criticism
Favors, asking and doing
Good wishes
Gratitude
Hesitation
How to talk
Meeting someone
Parting from someone
Proposals
Requests, Commands
Reserve
Responses
Special occasions, expressions for
Starting business discussions
Sympathy
Visiting

II. **WORDS & EXPRESSIONS** 153
Adjectives and adjectival expressions
Adverbs and adverbial expressions
Conjunctions and other linking expressions
Idiomatic expressions
Interjections
Onomatopoeic words and mimicry words
Particles and particle-like phrases
Personal terms
Sentence endings
Socially significant terms
Verbs and verbal expressions

III. **CUSTOMS & HABITS** 155
Customs and habits
Nonverbal expressions

IV. **MISCELLANEOUS** 156
Common mistakes
Pronunciation
Miscellaneous

I. SITUATIONAL EXPRESSIONS

Advice

. . . ta hoo-ga ii   V98-9, 146-7
. . . tara doo-desu-ka   V-12-3, 98-9

Apology

apologizing frequently   I30-1
apology for being a poor
   speaker   IV88-9
blaming oneself   I124-5
Doomo   I22-3
Doomo ki-ga tsukimasen-de   IV88-9
Doomo doomo   I23
Gomen-kudasai.   V90-1
Gomen-nasai vs. Shitsuree-
   shimashita   III14-5/III100-1
host's apology for taking the
   visitor's time   V30-1
Ki-ga tsukimasen-de,
   doomo.   IV88-9
Konna jikan-ni sumimasen. III124-5
Mooshiwake
   arimasen.   III100-1/V124-5
Ohikitome shimashite.   V30-1
Oisogashii tokoro-o . . .   III114-5
Ojama-shimasu.   I68-9
Ojama-shimashita.   I68-9
Omachidoosama.   III60-1
Omatase-shimashita.   III60-1
Osoreirimasu   I51
Senjitsu-wa shitsuree-
   shimashita.   I46-7
Shitsuree-desu-ga   V28-9
Shitsuree-shimasu.   I30-1/V90-1
Sumimasen   I51
Visitor's apology for taking
   the host's time   V30-1
Warui-desu-ne.   III100-1/V124-5

Asking about wishes

. . . de ii-desu-ka   V20-1
. . . shimashoo-ka   V54-5
. . . sureba yoroshii-deshoo IV54-5
. . . masen-ka   IV106-7

Daily greetings

Chotto soko-made.   I8-9
Dochira-e?   I8-9/IV91
Doomo   I22-3
Gochisoosama.   I54-5
Itadakimasu.   I54-5
Ja.   IV103
Ja, mata.   IV103
Konbanwa   I17, 63

Konnichiwa   I16-7, 63
Itadakimasu.   I54-5
Itte-(i)rasshai.   I62-3
Itte-mairimasu.   I62-3
Ohayoo-gozaimasu.   I17
Okaeri-nasai.   I62-3
Osaki-ni   IV62-3
Osomatsusama.   I54-5
Sayo(o)nara.   I68-9/II58-9/IV103
Shitsuree-shimasu.   V90-1
Tadaima.   I63

Disapproval, Criticism

Doo-deshoo-ne.   III28-9
Kore-mo kekkoo-desu-ga
. . .   IV118-9
Soo-deshoo-ka   V8-9
Taihen kekkoo-da-to
   omoimasu . . .   II116-7

Favors, asking and doing

ageru   IV24-5
. . . de ii-kara   III82-3
moratte-morau   IV24-5
Paying the bill for one's
   guest   V80-1
. . . te-kudasaru, . . . te-
   kureru   III30-1
. . . te-morau   II131
tsuide-ni   IV56-7
Yoroshiku.   IV120-1

Good wishes

Doozo goyukkuri.   III134-5
Rainen-ga yoi toshi-de
   arimasu yoo-ni.   II120-1
Sue-nagaku oshiawase-ni.   IV94

Gratitude

Arigatoo-gozaimasu.   II112-3
Arigatoo-gozaimashita.   II112-3
Benkyoo-ni narimashita.   I134-5
Doomo   I22-3
. . . ga osewa-ni natte-
   orimasu   I77
Gochisoosama.   I55
Gokuroosama.   I116-7
Maido arigatoo-gozaimasu.   V68-9
Okagesama-de   I72-3
oree   III120-1
osewa-ni naru   I77
Otsukaresama.   II42-3
Shujin-ga osewa-ni . . .   I77

Sumimasen vs. Arigatoo   I104-5
Tasukarimashita.   III132-3

Hesitation

anoo   I78-9
are-deshoo-ne   V88-9
Doo-deshoo-ne   V88-9
iinikui-n-desu-ga   II132-3
konna koto-o itte-wa nan-
  desu-ga   II146-7
saa . . .   II22-3
sounding hesitant   V88-9

How to talk

aizuchi   I14-5, 112-3/IV110/V47
answering a phone   V141
asking to repeat   IV110-1
avoiding mentioning one's
  own name   II168-9
avoiding using verbs   I66-7/V34-5
checking the listener's
  understanding   II70-1
complaint   I113
conversation opening   I132-3
expressing wishes
  indirectly   IV88-9
finishing up   IV84-5/V92-3, 145
identifying oneself with
  group members   II103
inside and outside
  the group   II142-3
inviting the listener to
  complete a statement   V47
leaving something unsaid
  after "doozo"   IV98-9
  after "kedo, kara"   II76-7
  after ". . . nai-to'"   II56-7
  after "nande"   IV66-7
  after "osaki-ni"   IV62-3
  after "yoroshiku"   IV120-1
  before "ii-ja arimasen-ka"   V20-1
  before ". . . temo ii"   IV18-9
  "doo-desu-ka" after ". . .
  tara"   V13
  leaving subject
    unsaid   V28-9, 40-1
  leaving verbs unsaid   II120-1
  when asking a favor   I97/IV100-1
  when giving negative
    evaluations   I96-7
  when wanting to be
    excused (Ee, chotto)   III112-3
leaving to the listener's
  judgment   III136-7
letting the listener choose   II13
men's speech vs. women's
  speech   V86-7, 18-9
mentioning one's own name   III168-9
monologue-like statement   II13

notion of what conversation
  should be   I15
opening remarks   IV92-3
polite vs.
  familiar   V24-5, 82-3, 118-9, 136-7
referring to common
  experience or
  feeling   I40-1/V144-5
refraining from praising
  superiors   V32-3
reporting someone's
  statement   V100-1
reversing the order of the
  subject and
  predicate   II54-5/V52-3
reversing word order   V52-3
signal words   I78-9/III8-9/IV34-5
speaker-listener distance   II136-7
stopgap phrases   I145/II60-1, 52-3
understanding an implicit
  message   IV88-9

Meeting someone

Gobusata-itashimashita.   I75/V102-3
Hajimemashite.   I123/II136-7
Hajimete ome-ni kakarimasu. IV82-3
Hisashiburi-desu-ne.   V102-3
Okaeri-nasai.   I62-3
Tadaima.   I63

Parting from someone

Bai-bai.   IV79
Gomen-kudasai.   V90-1
Itte-(i)rasshai   I62-3
Itte-kimasu.   I62-3
Itte-mairimasu.   I62-3
Ja, kore-de.   IV94-5
Sayo(o)nara.   I51, 62/II58-9/IV103
Shitsuree-shimasu.   V90-1

Proposals

. . . demo . . . masen-ka   I94-5
expressions of proposal   V22-3
hitotsu . . .   V14-5
ichido . . . tai   V14-5
Ii-ja arimasen-ka.   V20-1
Koko-wa watashi-ga . . .   V80-1
Konnano-de yokattara   III142-3
Makoto-ni tsumaranai mono-
  desu-ga   IV80-1
Omochi-shimashoo.   II136-7
Ookuri-shimashoo.   III134-5
Soo iwazu-ni (iwanaide)   IV100-1
Soo ossharazu-ni   IV100-1

Requests, Commands

expressions of request   V48-9, 94-5

hitotsu . . .   V14-5
ichido . . . tai   V14-5
Ki-ni shinai.   V142-3
Konna kanji-ni
   shite-kudasai.   III126-7
. . . koto.   V64-5
. . .n-da.   V64-5
. . . nai-de-ne.   V142-3
Onegai-shimasu.   I58-9/IV98-9
. . . te.   V48-9
. . . te-itadakemasen-
   deshoo-ka   V94-5
. . . te-itadakemasen-ka   V94-5
. . . te-kudasai.   V48-9, 94-5
. . . te-ne.   V142-3
Yoroshiku onegai-shimasu.   I58-9

Reserve

. . . de ii   V76-7
. . . de ii-kara   III82-3
. . . de kekkoo-desu-kara   II32-3
Itsu-demo ii-desu.   II40-1
. . . kamo shiremasen   V60-1
. . . kedo   III84-5
Maa-ne.   V32-3
refraining from expressing
   happiness   V30-1
reserved agreement   I123
reserved praise   V32-3

Responses

aizuchi   I14-5, 112-3/IV39, 110/V47
Chigaimasu.   V10-1
denying the other person's
   weak points   I10-1
Deshita.   V44-5
Desu.   V84-5
Desu-ne.   V92-3
Doo-itashimashite.   I75/III48-9
Doomo   I22
Doo-shita mon-deshoo-ne.   IV40-1
E?   II96-7/IV111
ee   V26-7
Ee, chotto.   III112-3/IV90
Ee, maa nantoka.   II156-7
Fun.   V110-1
Fun-fun.   V110-1
Ha.   V126-7
Ha?   II96-7
Hai.   II68-9/III58-9
Hai, hai.   V126-7
Hee?   V126-7
Hoo.   V110-1
Iie.   II10-1/III58-9
Iie, sonna koto-wa arimasen.   I10-1
Kochira-koso.   I74-5
Komarimashita-ne.   IV41
Otagaisama-desu.   I146-8
patience in listening to

someone's grumbling   IV40-1
responding to the speaker's
   intentions   II40-1/II50-1
Sekkaku-desu-kara . . .   III102-3
Soo-desu-ne . . .   I144-5
Taihen-desu-ne.   IV40-1

Special occasions, expressions for

Akemashite omedetoo-
   gozaimasu.   I52-3
condolences   II39
Doozo yoi otoshi-o.   I50-1
Kono tabi-wa tonda koto-de
   . . .   II105
ohiraki   IV94-5
Rainen-ga yoi toshi-de
   arimasu yoo-ni.   II120-1
Schochuu omimai
   mooshiagemasu.   V62-3
taboo words at weddings   94-5

Starting business discussions

De, kyoo-wa . . .?   III114-5
Jitsu-wa   I82-3/III102-3
. . . no koto-de chotto . . .   IV16-7
. . . no koto-desu-ga   IV17
sassoku-desu-ga   II140-1

Sympathy

expressions of sympathy II105/IV39
Goshuushoosama.   II105
Kikoo-no see-deshoo.   III32-3
Kono tabi-wa tonda koto-de
   . . .   II105
neighborly concern   I9/IV91
Odaiji-ni.   II105
Osabishii-deshoo-ne.   I142-3
response to expressions of
   sympathy   I142-3/III122-3
Sore-wa ikemasen-ne.   II105
sympathy with a complaint IV40-1
Taihen-desu-ne.   I64-5/IV40-1
Taishita koto-wa arimasen. III122-3
Uchi-wa motto hidoi-n-desu-
   yo.   I130-1
Zannen-desu-ne.   II104-5

Visiting

Chotto sono hen-made
   kimashita-node.   II110-1
Doozo goyukkuri.   III134-5
Gomen-kudasai.   V90-1
Irasshai.   V54-5
Irasshaimase.   III148-9/V54-5
leave-taking   I162-3
Oisogashii tokoro-o . . .   III114-5

II. WORDS & EXPRESSIONS

Adjectives and adjectival expressions

atsui vs. *atatakai*	II78
furui vs. *toshi-o totte-iru*	I108
joozu	V32-3
kanashisoo	I87
kekkoo	I138
komatta (hito)	II72-3
kowai	II144-5
mottainai	III10-1
muzukashii	II103
osoi vs. *osokatta*	V96-7
samui vs. *tsumetai*	I108-9
ureshisoo	I87
wakai	I102-3

Adverbs and adverbial expressions

amari	IV85
botsubotsu	IV28-9
chotto	I58, 96-7
doomo	IV85
doose	IV85
doozo	IV98-9
gossori	IV30-1
ichidomo	III106-7
issho-ni	V116-7
jimejime	III128-9
karari-to	III128-9
kekkyoku	I90-1
kesshite	III106-7/IV129
kiree-ni	V108-9
kondo	IV34-5
maido	V68-9
mata kondo	III118-9
nakanaka	III108-9/IV129
parapara	III128-9
sappari	IV30-1
sassoku	III104-5
sekkaku	III102-3
shitoshito	III128-9
sorosoro	IV28-9
sugu	III104-5
sukkari	IV30-1
tekitoo-ni	III136-7
tonikaku	III8-9
tootoo	I106
tsuide-ni	IV56-7
ukkari	II102
wazato	I98
wazawaza	I98/IV56-7
yappari	I90-1
yatto	I106
yoroshiku	IV120-1
zaazaa	III128-9

zuibun	V70-1

Conjunctions and other linking expressions

dakara	IV112-3
datte	II26-7
de	V18-9
. . . *dokoro-ka*	V128-9
. . . *ga*	I26-7
ja	II18-9
. . . *kara*	IV85
kawari-ni	IV26-7
. . . *kedo*	I26-7/IV85
. . . *node*	IV85
. . . *noni*	III192-3
shikashi	II28-9
sono kawari	IV26-7
sorede	V18-9
sorega	V36-7
sorekara	V18-9
sore-ni shitemo	III8-9
soshite	V18-9
. . . *tari* . . . *tari*	III116-7

Idiomatic expressions

. . . *bakari*	V112-3
. . . *dake-no koto-wa aru*	IV74-5
. . . *de ii*	II134
. . . *demo*	I94-5
. . . *dokoro-ka*	V128-9
. . . *eba ii-noni*	V98-9
. . . *eba yokatta-noni*	V66-7
. . . *hoo-ga ii*	V98-9
ii toshi (jikan)	V122-3
. . . *ka nanika*	I94-5
. . . *ki-ga suru*	III138-9
. . . *koto-ni naru*	II80-1/IV34-5
. . . *kuse-ni*	II124
. . . *mo* . . . *eba*	IV116-7
. . . *mon-desu*	IV68-9
. . . *mon(o)-ja nai*	II16-7
. . . *n-ja nakatta*	IV136-7
. . . *nanka*	II80-1
. . . *ni naru*	V58-9
. . . *ni totte*	V16-7
. . . *ni yoru-to*	IV46-7
. . . *ni yotte*	IV46-7
. . . *no koto-da-kara*	IV130-1
. . . *no koto-desu-ga*	V76-7
. . . *rashii*	II24-5
. . . *shika nai*	II110-1
. . . *soo (oishisoo)*	II88-9
. . . *te-miru*	I114
. . . *te shikata-ga nai*	V74-5
. . . *te shiyoo-ga nai*	V74-5

153

. . . te tamaranai	V74-5	niwa		V16-7
. . . to yuuno-wa	II46-7	ne	I56/IV122/V8-9	
. . . to yuu-to	II46-7	ne vs. yo		I56-7, 138-9
. . . tokoro-o	III114-5	no		III154-5
. . . ttara nai	IV72-3	no (sentence particle)		III146-7
. . . uchi-ni	IV22-3	o plus passive		V56-7
. . . wake-ja nai	III65-7, 84-5	sentence particles		II125/V86-7
. . . wake-niwa ikanai	II10-1	to		I98-9
. . . yoo-ni yuu	IV14-5	wa	III50-1, 90-1/V98-9, 104-5, 134-5	
. . . yoo-to suru	I114	wa vs. ga		III190-1
. . . wake-desu	I118-9	wa, sentence particle		II122-3
		yo		I37/V143

Interjections

		yone	V42-3
anoo	IV110	wayo	V42-3
bai bai	IV79	wayone	V43
ee . . .	II106-7		
hahaha	II66-7	**Personal terms**	
hai	I15, 112-3/III18-9/IV36-7		
hohoho	II66-7	aite	III12-3
hora	IV94-5	akachan vs. akanboo	V118-9
iie	I10-1	anata	I28-9
ja,	IV94-5	avoiding directly referring	
nee	IV122-3	to one's wife	V120-1
moshi-moshi	IV79	. . . chan	II138
naanda	V24-5	. . . dooshi	IV76-7
naruhodo	II20-1	hito	III22-3
oi	I58	kanai	V120-1
saa	II23	kanojo	IV20-1
		kare	IV20-1
		koohai	II46-7

Onomatopoeic words and mimicry words

		niisan	II138-9
		nyooboo	V120-1
		okusan	I29
burabura	I92-3/II86-7	okyakusama	V116-7
furafura	I92-3/II86-7	okyakusan	II48-9
gorogoro	I92-3	o . . . san	II84-5
jimejime	III128-9	oneesan	II138-9
karari-to	III128-9	onna	V114-5
korokoro	I93	onna-no-hito	II94-5
kosokoso	II86-7	otaku	III140-1
kotsukotsu	II86-7	otoko	V114-5
nikoniko	II86-7	. . . san	III30-1/IV96-7/V25
nitanita	II86-7	senpai	II139/III146-7
parapara	III128-9	shujin	IV20-1
shitoshito	III128-9	terms of respect	I60-1
sorosoro	I92-3	uchi-de	V120-1
ton ton	IV78-9	uchi-no yatsu	V120-1
zaazaa	III128-9		
zorozoro	I92-3	**Sentence endings**	

Particles and particle-like phrases

		. . . deshita-ne	II82-3
		. . . desho?	V82-3
		. . . desu	V84-5, 136-7
de	II134	. . . ja nai?	V132-3
demo	I94-5	. . . kamo shirenai	V60-1
different particles used by		. . . kashira	I128-9
men & women	V86-7	. . . kke	II83
ga	II134/III50-1, 90-1	. . . mase	V54-5
mo	II108-9/IV116-7	. . . mashite	V46-7
na	II12-3	. . . masu	V44-5
ni totte	V16-7	. . . mon-desu-ne	IV64-5

. . . n-desu	I100-1
. . . n-ja nai-deshoo-ka	I126
. . . soo-desu	V38-9
. . . te	V46-7
. . . tte	V40-1
. . . yoo-desu	III76-7, 110-1

Socially significant terms

byooki	III94-5
daiji	III144-5
guchi	IV38-9
mondai	IV16
ohiraki	IV94-5
okage	I72-3, 135
oree	III120-1
rikutsu	III120-1
tsukiai	III74-5
tsumori	IV52-3
uso	III70-1
yoso	III88-9

Verbs and verbal expressions

ageru	III62-3/IV24
aru	I33
causative	IV25
dekakeru	V106-7
deru	V106-7
future described by ". . .	
masu"	V38-9
gochisoo-suru	V80-1
iku	III78-9
irassharu	V130-1
iru	I33
kaeru	I58-9, 34-5
ki-ga suru	IV88-9
ki-ga tsuku	IV88-9
ki-ni naru	V73
ki-ni suru	V72-3, 142-3
kiku	IV38-9
kobosu	IV38-9
komaru	IV40-1, 70-1
kurasu	V106-7

kureru	II128-9
kuru	III178-9
miseru	IV12
modoru	I39
morau	II66-7
motte-kuru	I32-3
muri-o suru	III124-5
narau	IV128
neru	V114-5
oboeru	IV50-1
oitoma-suru	IV33
oshieru	IV12
otomo-suru	IV10-1
passive	I44-5
sasou	IV8
sewa-ni naru	V114-5
shiru	I56-7
. . . ta	II112-3/V146-7
. . . ta hoo-ga ii	V142-3
. . . ta used as a command	III116-7
. . . tai	I86-7
tanomu	IV8-9, 15
tasukeru	IV138-9
te form	V74-5
tetsudau	IV138-9
tomaru	V114-5
tooru	II66-7
tsurete-kuru	I32-3
verbs for asking	IV8
verbs for giving	II129/III62-3
verbs for receiving	II129
verbs for using only with	
human beings	V86-7
wakarimashita	IV104-5
wakaru	I56-7
wasureru	IV51
yaseru vs. yaseta	I34-5
. . . (y)oo-to suru	I114
. . . (y)oo-to omou	I88-9

(For . . . te followed by other
verbs as in "tabete-shimau," see
Index to Words, Phrases and
Sentences, P. 164)

III. CUSTOMS & HABITS

Customs and habits

admiration of foreigners'	
Japanese	IV86-7
answering for someone else	II64-5
avoiding having a	
guest help	V116-7
clumsy speech of influential	
statesman liked	V138-9
contact with others,	

maintaining	V102-3
distinction between formal	
and familiar expressions	
becoming looser	IV15
group consciousness	I17, 63
name cards	III168-9
ordering the same meal	V78-9
purposely complaining about	
one's weakness	V138-9
reserve towards foreigners	IV87

sending cards V62-3
tolerance of inadvertent
  mistakes II102

Nonverbal expressions

asking to move over II8-9
asking to repeat IV110
bodily expression of apology II38-9
bowing, how to bow IV82-3

gesture meaning "Excuse
  me" I19
handing over a gift IV81
hesitating before entering II48-9
knocking IV78-9
offering tea I66-7
speaker-listener distance II36-7
speaking while bowing IV82-3
sympathy II105
use of gestures I19

IV. MISCELLANEOUS

Common mistakes

classroom Japanese V116-7
imagoro vs. *konogoro* IV48-9
jikan-ga arimasu-ka I166
kaeru vs. *mata kuru* I38-9
naoru vs. *naosu* V34-5
nomitai-desu-ka I12-3
shirimasen vs. *wakarimasen* I56-7
shitsuree-desu-ga vs.
  shitsuree-shimasu V26-7
soo-deshoo-ne vs. *soo-*
  deshoo-ka V8-9
. . . *ta-kara* vs. . . . *te-kara* I106
. . . *temo* vs. . . . *eba* III52-3
transitive vs. intransitive
  verbs V34-5
tsukaimasu-ka IV106
wakarimasu IV105

Pronunciation

contraction I70-1/IV68-9, 72-3, 127
"*d*" sounding like "*r*" I99
dangling tone I27
"*i*" sound, dropping of I102/II78-9
long and short
  vowels I42-3, 107/II168-9
"*m*" sound II35
nasalized "*g*" sound I27
"*n*" sound, syllabic I109
"*o*" sound,
  dropping of II134-5/IV124-5
prominence I48-9/III90-1
stops (double *t*) I115/II78-9/IV140-1
successive vowels II118-9
"*w*" sound II34-5
"*t*" sound, dropping of IV140-1

Miscellaneous

agreeing before criticizing II16-7
approximate amount I20-1

avoid saying no III84-5
classroom Japanese V117
complete sentence, concept
  of I120-1
customer not responding to
  greeting V54-5
declining someone's offer IV18-9
devaluation IV142-3
dialects II144-5
double negation IV60-1
emphasis V50-1, 56-7
ending of meetings IV94-5
ending of telephone
  conversation IV103
familiar commands V48-9, 142-3
future tense V44-5
giving a message V100-1
inquiring after health I24-5
irritation V50-1
kono vs. *sono* V100-1
laughter, description of II66-7
leaving early IV63
loan words III98-9
. . . *ni naru* as a polite
  expression V58-9
partial negation V134-5
play on words III64-5, 72-3, 86-7
proverbs III80-1
quarreling III142-3
quotation III100-1
railway announcements II44-5
reading of numerals III86-7
reasons for being excused III195
regret II104-5
self-assertion II63/IV32-3
source of information,
  specifying IV46-7
surprise III36-7
trying to recall something IV51
words meaning two different
  things I138/V114-5
words that should not be
  used at weddings IV94-5

INDEX TO WORDS, PHRASES AND SENTENCES

Volumes 1-5

A

Aa, soo (yuu wake)-ka.	I84-5/II21
A, atta, atta.	I127
ageru	I20, 97/III62-3
aite	III12-3
aite-ni suru	III13
aizuchi	I15/IV39/V47
aizuchi-no uchikata	I112-3
akachan vs. *akanboo*	V118-9
Akemashite omedetoo-gozaimasu.	I52-3
anata	I28-9
ano-ne	I79
anoo	I78-9/II106-7
apology (nonverbal)	II38-9
apology for being a poor speaker	IV92-3
are (Are-o motte-kite)	I40-1
are-deshoo-ne	V88-9
Arigatoo-gozaimashita.	II112-3
. . . (s)asete-itadaku	IV25
asking to move over (nonverbal)	II8-9
asking to repeat	IV96-7
atatakai vs. *atsui*	II78
ato-de kekkoo-desu-kara	II32-3
Atsuku narimashita-ne.	I100-1
azukaru	I82

B

baibai	IV79
bakari (sen-en-bakari)	I20-1/V12-3
Benkyoo-ni narimashita.	I134-5
biyooin vs. *byooin*	I107
botsubotsu	IV28-9
botsubotsu vs. *sorosoro*	IV28-9
bowing	II39/IV82-3
burabura vs. *buruburu*	I187
Burabura shite-imashita.	I92-3
byooki	III194-5

C

. . . chan	II138
. . . chan vs. *. . . san*	II143
. . . chatta	IV126-7
. . . chatta (Mata shippai-shichatta)	I122
checking the listener's understanding	II70-1
Chigaimasu.	V10-1
chiisai toki	I103
chooshi-ga warui	III14-5

chotto	I58
Chotto . . .	I96-7
Chotto sono hen-made kimashita-node . . .	II110-1
Chotto tsugoo-ga warui-node . . .	III95
Chotto yooji-ga atte . . .	III95
classroom Japanese	V116-7
complaining about one's health	III14-5
complimenting the host	V32
condolences	II39
counters	II98-9
criticizing politely	III117

D

"*d*" sound (*Edo* vs. *ero*)	I99
daiji-ni suru	III144-5
dakara	IV112-3
dake	IV75
. . . dake-no koto-wa aru	IV75
. . . de itte-imashita	IV45
. . . de yonda	IV47
dake (sanjippun-dake)	I110-1
datte	II26-7
. . . de ii vs. *. . . ga ii*	II134
. . . de ii-desu	V22-3, 76-7
. . . de ii-kara	II182-3
. . . de irasshaimasu	V130-1
De, kyoo-wa . . .?	II114-5
. . . de yokattara	III142-3
Dekinai wake-ja arimasen-kedo . . .	III84-5
demo (Ocha-demo nomimasen-ka)	I94-5
Demo amari osoku naru-to . . .	II56-7
Demo, moo naremashita.	I143
Demo ojama-deshoo-kara.	I149
denwa-ga kakatte-kuru	V141
Denwa-ga tookute yoku kikoemasen.	III147
deru vs. *dekakeru*	V106-7
. . . deshita-ne	I183
. . . desho(o)?	V82-3
. . . desu used for explaining and reporting	V84-5
Desu, Deshoo, Deshita used as an answer	V144-5
. . . desu-mono	I127
. . . desu-ne	II52-3
Desu-ne used as an answer	V92-3
. . . desu-no	III147
dewa	II118-9

dialects	II144-5
Dochira-e?	I8-9/II111/IV91
Doita, doita.	III17
. . . dokoro-ka	V128-9
. . . domo	III197
Donata-deshita-ka.	II83
Doo-deshoo-ne.	III28-9
Doo-desu-ka.	I24
Doo-itashimashite.	I75/III48-9
Doo omoimasu-ka.	III29
Doo shita mon-deshoo-ne.	IV40
Dooka-to omoimasu.	III29
doomo	I22-3/II190/III149
Doomo ojama-shimashita.	I69
Doomo shitsuree-shimashita.	I30
doose	II74-5, 90
. . . dooshi	IV76-7
Dooyara kooyara.	I137
doozo	I66-7/II9/IV98-9
Doozo vs. Onegai-shimasu	IV98-9
Doozo goyukkuri.	III134-5
Doozo oagari-kudasai.	II49
Doozo odaiji-ni.	I51/III44
Doozo ogenki-de.	I51
Doozo oki-o tsukete.	I51
Doozo yoi otoshi-o (omukae-kudasai)	I50-1
Doozo yoroshiku.	I75/II136
dore	I40
dropping of the "i" sound	IV141
double negative	IV61

E

E?	IV111
. . . eba	IV116
. . . eba vs. . . . temo	III53
. . . eba ii-noni	V98-9
Ee.	II112/III58-9
ee, anoo, eeto	II106-7
Ee, chotto.	III112-3/IV90
Ee, chotto soko-made.	I8, 25
Ee, ee.	I14
Ee, honjitsu-wa . . .	II106-7
Ee, maa-ne.	I123
eeto	I145
expressions of sympathy	IV40-1
expressions used for introducing oneself	III68-9
expressions used in the classroom	IV110-1

F

family terms, use of	II138-9
finishing up someone's statement	IV84-5
Furafura shite-imashita.	I92-3
furareta (passive)	I45
furisoo vs. furu-soo	II89

furui vs. toshi-o totte-iru	I108
future action	V39

G

"g" sound (in kagi, nasalized)	I127
ga vs. wa	III150-1
ga (Watashi-desu-ga . . .)	I26-7
. . . (desu) ga, . . .	IV132-3
. . . ga ii	III190-1
. . . ga itta-n-desu-ga	IV47
. . . ga soo mooshimasu (iimasu)-node . . .	III26-7
Ganbaranakucha.	I71
garasu vs. gurasu	III199
. . . gata	III197
give, words meaning	II162-3
giving advice	V98-9
gobenkyoo-chuu	III125
Gobusata-itashimashita.	I75/V102-3
Gochisoosama(-deshita).I54-5/III149
gochisoo-suru	V80
Gokuroosama.	I116-7
gomen-nasai	II14-5/III101
gomennasai vs. sumimasen	II15
gorogoro	I93
(. . . kara) goshookai-itadaita mono-desu	III68-9
gossori	IV30-1
Gotaikutsusama-deshita.	I143
gozonji	I57
guchi	IV38-9
guchi-o kobosu	IV38-9
guchi-o yuu	IV38-9
. . . gurai (Soo-ne, mittsu-gurai)	I20-1

H

Ha?	IV110-1
haa	II14-5
ha ha ha	II166-7
hai	I15, 112-3/IV36-7
hai used to show finality	III18-9
hai vs. iie	II69/III58-9
Hai, orimasen.	II68-9
hairu vs. ireru	V35
Hajimemashite.	I132/II136
Hajimemashite. Doozo yoroshiku.	I75
Hajimete ome-ni kakarimasu.IV82-3
Hakusen-no uchigawa-e sagatte omachi-kudasai.	II45
handing over a gift	IV80-1
Hayai-desu-ne.	I36
having the same meal	V78-9
hazu	IV144-5
Hisashiburi-desu-ne.	V102-3
hissing sound used when starting a statement	II107

hito	III22-3, 80
hitoyama	II98-9
hito-yasumi	III131
Hitotsu ikaga-desu-ka	III131
ho ho ho	III66-7
hodo	I20-1
hoken-o kakete-oku	II93
homerareru	IV126-7
Honnen-mo doozo yoroshiku	
onegai-itashimasu.	I53
Honno hitotsu-desu-ga . . .	III163
Honto.	III71
hora	IV36-7

I

Ichinichi-mo hayaku ogenki-ni	
nararemasu yoo-ni.	II121
ichioo (Ichioo oazukari-	
shimasu)	I82-3
Ii-desu.	IV18-9
Ii-desu-ne.	V124-5
Ii-ja arimasen-ka.	V20-1
ii jikan	V123
ii toshi	V122-3
Iie.	I10-1/V10-1
Iie, honno sukoshi-de . . .	II50-1
Iie, motomoto chooshi-ga	
yoku nakatta-n-desu-kara	
. . .	I124
Iie, tondemo arimasen.	III123
iinikui	II132-3
Ikaga-desu-ka.	I24-5
Ikoo-ka-to omoimasu.	I89
iku vs. kuru	III78-9
ima-goro	IV48-9
ima-goro vs. kono-goro	IV48-9
Ima nanji-deshoo-ka.	I166
ima-no uchi-ni asonde-oku	II113
inaku narimashita vs.	
nakunarimashita	I102
incomplete sentences as	
polite inquiries	II124
indirect expressions of	
disapproval	IV118-9
intransitive verb + te-imasu	
vs. transitive verb + te-	
arimasu	III140-1
introduction	II64-5
introductory remarks	IV133
inversion of phrases	I54-5
ippai nomu	III130-1
Irasshai.	III134/V54-5
Irasshaimase.	I17/III149/V54-5
irasshaimasu	I29
iru vs. aru	I33
isogeba vs. isoidemo	II153
Issho-ni doo?	II103
issho-ni . . . suru	V116-7
Itadakimasu.	I54-5
Itsudemo ii-desu.	I140-1

itsumo-no yoo	V69
Itte-(i)rasshai.	I51, 62/II59
Itte-kimasu.	I62/II58
Itte-mairimasu.	I62/II58
iya	II51

J

ja	II18-9, 59
Jaa, kore-de.	I71
Ja, itte-rasshai.	I25
Ja, kore-de.	II59/IV95
Ja, kyoo-wa kore-de.	II59
Ja, mata.	II59/IV103
. . . ja nai(-ka)	V132-3
jimejime	III128-9
jitsu-ni	I81
jitsu-wa	I80-1/II102-3, 140
jiyuu vs. juu	I107
joozu	V32-3

K

ka (Ikoo-ka-to omoimasu)	I89
ka nanika (suugaku-ka	
nanika)	I95
Kaeranakereba narimasen.	IV32
Kaeranakucha.	I70-1
kaeri-de ii-kara	III82-3
kaetta toki	I35
Kaettara sugu denwa-	
shimasu.	I120-1
Kaette-kudasai.	I38-9
. . . kamo shiremasen	V60-1
kanai	V120-1
kankee-ga aru	V114-5
kanojo	IV20-1
karada-o kowasu	III124
karari-to (karatto)	III128-9
kare	IV20-1
karuta	V16
kashira (Dekiru-kashira)	I128-9
kata	III123
Katta, katta.	III116-7
kawari (-ni)	IV26-7
kedo (Hai, orimasu-kedo	
. . .)	I26-7
. . . kedo vs. . . . kara	II76-7
kekkon-suru hito	I35
kekkon-suru koto-ni	
narimashita	II80-1
Kekkoo-desu.	I138/IV19
Kekkoo-desu-ne.	I138
kekkyoku	I90-1/II74-5
. . . keredomo	III92-3
kesshite	III106-7/IV129
. . . (yoona) ki-ga suru	III138-9
ki-ga tsukimasen-de . . .	IV88-9
Ki-o tsukenakucha ikemasen-	
ne.	I37

Ki-o tsukenakucha ikemasen-
yo. I37
kibun-ga warui III94
Kikimasen. III146-7
kikoeru vs. kiku III146-7
kikoo-no see III32
kiku III146-7/IV8
kimasu vs. kite-imasu I102
kimochi-ga warui III94
ki-ni naru V73
Ki-ni shinai. V142-3
ki-ni suru V72-3
Kinoo-wa yoku furimashita-
ne. I100
kiree-ni V108-9
kitatte vs. kittatte II79
kite-kudasai vs. kitte-kudasai I115
kite-kure-to iwaremashita II101
. . . kke I183
knocking IV78-9
kobosu IV38-9
Kochira-koso. I74-5, 76
kodomo-no toki I103
Koko-de shitsuree-shimasu. III35
Koko-de tomete-kudasai. I48-9
Komarimashita-ne. IV40-1
Komarimasu-ne. IV70-1
komatta hito II73
Komatta-na. II12-3
Konbanwa. I17
kondo IV34-5
konna fuu III127
konna guai III127
konna jikan-ni III124-5
Konna kanji-ni shite-
kudasai. III126-7
konna koto-o onegai-shite-wa
nan-desu-kedo II146
konnano-de yokattara III142-3
Konnichiwa. I16-7
kono vs. sono V100-1
kono-goro IV48-9
kono tabi IV35
Kono tabi-wa tonda koto-de
. . . II105
koohai III44-5
Koo yuu mono-desu. III68-9
kore I40
Kore-mo kekkoo-desu-ga
. . . IV118-9
Kore-wa ii-desu vs. Kore-ga
ii-desu III90-1
korokoro I93
. . . koto-ni narimashita IV34-5
koto-ni naru vs. koto-ni suru II80-1
kotsukotsu vs. kosokoso II87
kowai II144-5
Kowaremashita. I125
Kowashimashita. I124-5
kowashite-arimasu III140-1
. . . kun IV96

kurasu V107
kureru vs. ageru II128-9
kurikuri vs. kurakura II87
kuru vs. iku III78-9
kuru yoo-ni iwaremashita II101
. . . kuse-ni II24-5
kusuri-o nondemo III52-3
kyan kyan II167
Kyoo-wa . . . deshita-ne. II82-3
Kyoo-wa donna fuu-ni
shimashoo-ka. V68-9
Kyoo-wa nanika . . . II115

L

leave-taking II62-3
leaving out the subject of a
sentence V28-9
leaving the concluding part
unsaid II56-7
loan words III98-9

M

"m" sound II35
maa IV134-5
maa (Maa-ne) I123
machigatte-iru-kamo
shiremasen-ga II116-7
mada-mada (lie, mada-mada-
desu) I136
Maido arigatoo-
gozaimasu. III149/V68-9
Maido gojoosha arigatoo-
gozaimasu. II43
mairimasu III70
Makoto-ni tsumaranai mono-
desu-ga . . . IV80-1
. . . masen-ka IV106-7
. . . masen-ka vs. . . . masu-
ka IV115-6
. . . mashite . . . V46-7
. . . masu used for future V44
mata IV66-7
Mata kite-kudasai. I39
mata kondo III118-9
medetai III173
mimesis II86-7
minna vs. minnano III54-5
miru vs. mieru III147
mo (ningen-mo) III109
. . . mo suru IV116-7
Modotte-kimasu. I39
. . . mon-desu II16-7
. . . mon(o)-desu-ne IV64-5
. . . mon-ja arimasen II16-7
mondai IV16
mono III22-3
Moo ichido itte-
kudasai. II96-7/IV110-1
Moo kaeranakucha. I70

160

moo sorosoro dekakenai-to	II56-7
mookaru vs. moo kaeru	II118-9
moratte-morau	IV24-5
morau	II67
moshimoshi	IV79, 102-3
mottainai	III10-1, 145
Motte-kimasu.	I32-3
Muri-desu-wa.	II122-3
muri-o suru	IV24-5
murina onegai	III25
mushiatsui	III129
muzukashii	II102

N

"n" sound (niman-en vs. niman-nen)	I109
. . . n-da used as a command	V64-5
n-desu (Isogashii-n-desu-ka)	I100-1
. . . n-desu-ka	IV108-9
. . . n-ja nai	IV137
. . . n-ja nai?	I126
. . . n-ja nai-deshoo-ka	I126
. . . n-ja nakatta	IV137
na (Komatta-na.)	II12, 123
naanda	V24-5
Naani?	IV112
. . . nai uchi-ni	IV22-3
nakanaka	III108-9
nakareta (passive)	I44-5
. . . nakereba narimasen	IV33
Nan-da-tte?	IV111
. . . nan-desu-ga, nan-desu-kedo	II146-7
nande mata . . .	IV66-7
Nandemo ii-desu.	I141
Nanimo gozaimasen-ga doozo.	I54
Nanimo okamai-dekimasen-de . . .	V30
nanji-deshoo-ka	II66
. . . nanka	II90-1
nanka (Boku-nanka dame-desu-yo)	I136
. . . nanka vs. . . . wa	II91
nantettatte	II79
nan-to iimasu-ka	I60-1
nan-to mooshimashoo-ka	II61
nan-to-naku	III139
nan-to yuu-ka(na)	II61
nantoka (Ee, maa, nantoka)	I136-7
naoru vs. naosu	V34-5
narareta (byooki-ni narareta, passive)	I45
narau	IV128-9
narau vs. oboeru	IV128-9
naruhodo	II20-1
Naruhodo-nee.	I85/II21
Nasake-wa hito-no tame-narazu	III80-1

ne (Soo-desu-ne)	II123
ne added to . . .te	V143
ne vs. yo	I36-7, 138-9
neage-suru koto-ni narimashita	II81
nee	IV122-3/V8
netsu-ga aru	III95
. . . ni vs. . . . niwa	V16-7
. . . ni kaite-atta	IV47
. . . ni kiita-n-desu-ga . . .	IV47
. . . ni naranakereba . . . masen	IV60-1
. . . ni narimasu	V58-9
. . . ni totte	V17
. . . ni yoru-to	IV46-7
. . . ni yoru-to vs. . . . ni yotte	IV46-7
. . . ni yotte	IV46-7
Nihon-wa nagai-desu-ka.	I133
Nihongo-ga ojoozu-desu-ne.	II132-3
Nihon-ryoori-wa taberaremasu-ka.	I133
niisan-to oneesan	II138-9
nikoniko vs. nitanita	II86-7
. . . nikui	II132-3
. . . niwa itsumo osewa-ni natte-orimasu	III31
no added at the end of a sentence	III46-7
. . . no koto-de chotto	IV16-7
. . . no koto-desu-ga . . .	V17
. . . no koto-da-kara	IV130-1
. . . node vs. . . . kara	II33
no-ne (Aa, kyoo-wa isogashii-no-ne)	I128
. . . noni	III92-3
noyone	V43
numbers, position of	III54-5
numerals, reading of	III86-7
Nyooboo-nimo kikasete-yaritai-to omoimashita.	I135

O

. . . o + passive	V56-7
o, polite prefix	II84-5
"o" sound, pronun. of	IV124-5
o-ari vs. owari	II34-5
Oashimoto-ni gochuui-kudasai	II44-5
Obaachan, koko-e kakenasai-yo.	I129
obaasan	I60
obasan vs. obaasan	I43
oboeru	IV50-1
oboete-iru	IV50-1
Ocha-demo ikaga-desu-ka.	I13
Ocha-demo nomimasen-ka.	I90-1
Ocha-ga hairimashita-kara doozo.	II32-3

Ocha-ga hairimashita-kedo
. . . II76-7
Ocha-o doozo. I66-7
Odaiji-ni. II105
Odekake-desu-ka. I25/III113/IV90-1
ogoru V80
ohanashi-chuu III125
Ohayoo-gozaimasu. I17
Ohikitome-shimashite . . . V30-1
ohiraki IV94-5
Oi. I58
o-isha-san II84-5
oishisoo II88-9
oite-oite-kudasai II92-3
oisogashii tokoro-o III115
Oitoma-shimasu. IV33
ojama V30
Ojama-shimasu. I68-9/III79
Ojama-shimashita. I68
ojama-shitai-n-desu-ga . . . III79
Ojama-shite-imasu. III135
ojiisan I60
Ojikan-o torimashite . . . V30
ojisan I60
ojisan vs. *ojiisan* I43
okaasan I29
Okaerinasai. I63
okage II133
okagesama-de I72-3, 74-5
*Okagesama-de yoku
  wakarimashita.* I135
*Okuchi-ni aimasen-deshoo-
  ga.* I125
*Okuni-wa dochira-
  desu-ka.* I133/II64-5
okusan I29
Okusan-mo iku? I29
okuru III134-5
okutte-kuru III138-9
okyakusama VI16-7
Omachidoosama. III160-1
Omatase-itashimashita. II42
Omatase-shimashita. III160-1
*Omedetoo-
  gozaimasu.* I143/II104/III173
omochi-shimashoo II126-7
omochi-shimashoo vs. *motte-
  agemashoo* II136
omoshiroi II73
onaka-o kowasu II194
oneesan I60-1
Onegai-shimasu. I58-9
*(Yamada-san-o)onegai-shima-
  su.* I49
oniisan I60
onna V114-5
onna vs. *onna-no-hito* IV94-5
onna-no kuse-ni II24-5
onna-rashii II24-5
oree III120-1
oree-no shirushi-ni III121

Osabishii-deshoo-ne. I142-3
Osaki-ni. II92/IV62-3
osewa-ni naru I76/V114-5
Osewasama. III149
oshieru IV12-3
oshieru vs. *miseru* IV12-3
oshiete-kureru II130-1
oshiete-morau II131
oshigoto-chuu III125
Oshigoto-wa doo-desu-ka. I73
oshokuji-chuu III125
Osomatsusama-deshita. I55
Osoreirimasu. I31/II135
osoreirimasu-ga I79
otagai-ni I146-8
Otagaisama-desu. I146-8
otaku III140-1
otaku-no minasan III140
Otaku-wa ii hoo-desu-yo. I131
otearai vs. *otera* III118-9
otetsudai-sasete-kudasai III143
otomo-suru IV10-1
otoko V114-5
otoko vs. *otoko-no-hito* I194-5
otsukare-no tokoro-o III115
Otsukaresama-deshita. I142-3
owari IV94-5
Owasuremono-no nai yoo-ni. I144-5
oyaku-ni tachimasen-de III133

P

parapara III129
partial negation III156-7
passive form (*nakareta*,,
  etc.) I44-5/IV126-7
phrases that can be said
  backwards III164-5
piinattsu vs. *nankinmame* III198-9
plain form used in quoted
  parts II101
plain negative used as a
  command V142-3
polite expressions used by
  foreigners IV86-7
polite speech used to show
  distance III142-3
position of phrases
  indicating numbers IV125

R

"*r*" sound II35
*Rainen-ga yoi toshi-de
  arimasu yoo-ni* II120-1
raisu vs. *kome* III198
. . . *rashii* II24-5
readings of numerals II186-7
remember IV50-1

response toward the
intention or wish rather
than the verbal meaning II87
reversing word order V52-3
rikutsu-o yuu III20-1

S

sa (sentence particle) II123
saa . . . II22-3
Saa, dekakemashoo. I123
Saa, doo-deshoo-ne. II22-3
*Sakunen-chuu-wa iroiro
osewa-ni narimashita.* I53
. . . *sama* II138
samuke-ga suru III195
Samuku narimashita-ne. I36
. . . *san* I18-9/II138/IV96/V25
. . . *san* added to the names
of companies III30-1
. . . *san-tachi* II196-7
sappari IV31
. . . *(s)asete-itadaku* IV25
sashiageru II121/III162
sasou IV8-9
sassoku III104-5
sassoku-de osoreirimasu-ga II141
sassoku-desu-ga II140-1
Sayo(o)nara I51, 63/II58-9/IV103
see III132-3
sekkaku-dakara III102-3
*Sekkaku oide-
kudasaimashita-noni* . . . III193
senpai II139/III144-5
*Senjitsu-wa gochisoosama-
deshita.* I46-7
*Senjitsu-wa shitsuree-
shimashita.* I46-7
sensee I61, 98/II139
sentence particles II123
sentence particles used by
men and women V86-7
(kaera)sete-itadakimasu III142-3
*Shachoo-mo irasshaimasu-
ka.* I29
Shachoo-wa orimasen. II142-3
*shika (Sanjippun-shika
arimasen)* I110-1
shikashi II28-9
shiken-ni toorimashita I167
shinareta (passive) I45
shinde-imasu vs. *shinisoo-
desu* II106
*Shinnen omedetoo-
gozaimasu.* I50, 53
shinpai-suru V72-3
Shirimasen. I56-7
shitoshito III129
*shitsuree(-shimasu,
-shimashita)*
I30-1, 51, 69/II15/IV62-3, 103

Shitsuree-shimasu. vs.
Shitsuree-desu-ga. V26-7
shochuu-mimai (joo) V62-3
Soo-deshoo-ka. V8-9
Soo-deshoo-ne. V8-9
Soo-desu-ka. V9
Shooshoo omachi-kudasai. II42
shufu vs. *shuufu* I42
shujin vs. *shuujin* I42-3
*Shujin-ga itsumo osewa-ni
natte-orimasu.* I76-7
soba III172
*sonna koto-o yuu mon-ja
arimasen* II16-7
Sonna koto-wa arimasen-yo. I37
sono-gurai IV142-3
sono hen II111
*Sono hen-made ookuri-
shimashoo.* III35
sono kawari IV26-7
sono-kurai IV142-3
sono uchi IV58-9
Sono yoo-desu. III110-1
. . . *soo* vs. *mieru* II88-9
Soo iwanaide . . . IV100-1
Soo ossharazu-ni . . . IV100-1
*Soo yuu wake-nimo
ikimasen-yo.* II10-1
Soo-da-ne. I145
Soo-deshoo-ne. I14
Soo-desu-ka. I14
Soo-desu-ne(e) I144-5/II116/III184-5
Soo-ka. I84-5
Soo-ne(e). I145
soo (ureshisoo) I87
sore I40-1
sore-dake IV74-5
sorede V18-9
sore-ga V36-7
sore-ja II19
sore-ni shite-mo II124-5
Sore-wa arigatoo-gozaimasu. III136
Sore-wa chotto . . . II185
sore-wa desu-ne II152-3
Sore-wa ikemasen-ne. I130
sore-wa soo-to II140
Sore-wa sore-wa. III136-7
Sorehodo-demo arimasen. III123
sorosoro I92-3/IV29
Sorosoro oitoma-shimasu. I71
Sorosoro shitsuree-shimasu. IV32
soshite V18-9
speaker-listener distance II136-7
stopgap phrases II60-1
sugu III104
sukkari IV31
sukoshi-mo III107
*Sukoshi tsumete-
kudasaimasen-ka.* II8-9
Sumimasen. I104-5/III100
sumimasen-ga I79/II9

. . . sureba yoroshii-deshoo IV54-5
sympathy, expressions of   IV40-1
sympathy for sickness   III14-5

T

. . . ta (passive form of
  verbs)   I34-5
. . . ta vs. dictionary form
  of adjectives   V96-7
. . . ta used to indicate a
  command   III17/V142-3
. . . ta used to show
  completion of an action III17
. . . ta hoo-ga ii   V98-9, 146-7
. . . ta tsumori   IV52-3
. . . tachi   III96-7
Tadaima.   I63
tagai   I146
tagaru (ikitagaru)   I86-7
tai (nomitai, ikitai)   I13, 86-7
Taihen tame-ni narimashita. I135
Taihen-desu-ne.   I64-5/II105/IV40-1
(Shufu-wa)taihen-desu-ne. I42
(Kinoo-wa)taihen-deshita. I65
Taihen kekkoo-da-to
  omoimasu.   II116-7
Taishita koto-wa arimasen. III112-3
tame   III133
tanomu   IV8, 14
tanoshii hito   II72-3
. . . tara used to show
  irritation   V50-1
. . . tara doo(-desu-ka)   V98-9
. . . tara ikaga-deshoo   V147
tari (Ocha-o nondari . . .) I99
. . . tari . . . tari suru III116-7
Tasukarimashita.   III132-3
tasukaru vs. tasukeru   III132
tasukeru   IV138
. . . te used as a command V48-9
. . . te-ageru   IV25
. . . te-iku   IV44-5
. . . te-imasu   V38-9, 45
. . . te-imasu vs. -soo-desu II126-7
. . . te-itadaku   IV25
. . . te-itte-kudasai   IV146-7
. . . te-kara vs. . . . takara I107
. . . te-kimasu   II30-1
. . . te-kudasai   V94-5
. . . te-kudasaru vs. . . . te-
  itadaku   IV114-5
. . . te-kurereba yokatta-noni V66-7
. . . te-kureru, . . . te-
  kudasaru   II130-1
. . . te-kuru
               IV42-3/III28-9/V29, 140-1
. . . te-miru (kekkon-shite-
  mimashita-ga)   I114
. . . te-morau   II131

. . . te-oku   II92-3
. . . te shikata-ga nai   V74-5
. . . te-shimau   IV126-7
. . . te shiyoo-ga nai   V74-5
. . . te tamaranai   V74-5
Tekitoo-ni yatte-kudasai. III136-7
. . . temo   II93
. . . te-mo ii   V110-1
terms of respect   IV96-7
tetsudau vs. tasukeru   IV138-9
. . . te-wa ikaga-deshoo   V147
to (Ocha-to okashi-o . . .) I99
. . . to omoimasu   I88-9/III179
to yuu-to   II46-7
to yuu-to vs. to yuu-nowa II46-7
. . . tokoro   III114
tokoro-de   II140
tomaru vs. neru   V114-5
tonton   IV78-9
tone (KOKO-DE tomete-
  kudasai)   I48-9
tonikaku   III8-9
Tonikaku yatte-mimashoo.   II9
tootoo   I106
toshi-o totte-iru vs. furui I108
tsuide-ni   IV56-7
tsukareyasui   III15
tsukiai   III74-5
Tsumaranai
  mono-desu-ga.   I125/III62-3
tsumetai vs. samui   I109
tsumori   IV52-3
tsurete-kuru vs. motte-kuru I32-3
. . . ttara nai   IV72-3
. . . ttara vs. . . . tte IV73
. . . tte   IV68-9/V40-1
"tte" sound   IV140-1

U

uchi-e kaetta toki   I35
. . . uchi-ni   IV22-3
uchi-no kaisha   III88
Uchi-wa motto hidoi-n-desu-
  yo.   II30-1
ukagaimasu   III79
ukkari   II102
understanding an implicit
  message   IV88-9
unten vs. doraibu   III199
use of desu and masu   V136-7
use of wa   V134-5
Uso.   III70-1

V

verbs ending in . . . ta or
  . . . da   II113
vowels, length of   I42-3, 107
vowels, successive   II119

W

"*w*" sound	II34-5
wa (Muri-desu-wa.)	II122-3
wa vs. *ga*	III90-1
. . . *wa* vs. . . . *mo*	II109
. . . *wa* . . . *da*	V104-5
wakai toki vs. *chiisai toki*	I102
Wakarimasen.	I56-7
Wakarimashita, hai.	III18-9
Wakarimashita-ka.	II70-1
Wakarimasu.	IV105
Wakarimasu-ka.	II70-1
wakatte-imasu	IV104-5
Wakatte-imasu vs.	
Wakarimashita	IV104-5
wake (. . . *wake-desu*)	I118-9
. . . *wake-ja arimasen*	III56-7
. . . *wake-ja arimasen-kedo*	III184-5
. . . *wake-niwa ikanai*	II10-1
wanwan	III67
Warui(-desu)-ne.	I31/III100-1/V124-5
Warui-wane.	III101
watashi	I120-1
. . . *wayone*	V43
waza-to	I98
wazawaza	I98/IV57
word play	III86-7
words meaning "give"	III62-3
words that can be said backwards	III64-5

Y

yappari	I90-1/II75
yaru	III162
yaseru vs. *yaseta*	I34-5
Yasumasete-itadakimasu	III42
Yasumono-desu-yo, konnano.	I10
yasumu wake-niwa ikanai	II10-1
yatto vs. *tootoo*	I106
yo (. . . *desu-yo*)	I36-7/II123
yo added to . . . *te*	V143
yoi . . . o	I50-1
Yokatta-desu-ne.	II104
Yokattara kite-kudasai.	I115
Yoku irasshaimashita.	III134/V55
yoku kite-kuremashita, -kudasai.	II131
yonde-mite-itadakemasu-ka	II31
. . . *yone*	V42-3
. . . *yoo (kekkon-shiyoo-to shimashita)*	I114
. . . *yoo-desu*	III76-7, 100-1
. . . *yoo-ni*	II120-1
. . . *yoo-ni omoimasu*	III111
. . . *yoo-ni yuu*	IV14-5
. . . *yoona ki-ga suru*	III138-9
yoroshikattara	III143
Yoroshikattara meshiagatte-kudasai.	II163
Yoroshiku onegai-shimasu.	I59
yoso	III88-9
yosoiki, yosoyuki	II189
yosoyososhii	II189
Yuremasu-kara gochuui-negaimasu.	II44-5

Z

zaazaa furu	III129
Zannen-desu-ne.	II104-5
zenryaku	II141
zenzen	III107
zo (. . . *da-zo.*)	II123
zorozoro	I93
zuibun	V70-1